THE 1%
SOLUTION

FOR WORK AND LIFE

More Acclaim for *The 1% Solution for Work and Life*

"Bad habits are easy to come by and hard to live with; good habits are hard to come by and easy to live with. If you put Tom's proven steps to work, success will follow."
Rodger Ford, Founder, AlphaGraphics, Chief Executive Officer, SynCardia Systems

"The principles put forth in *The 1% Solution for Work and Life* are straightforward, practical, and infinitely doable. The storytelling is compelling and the situations real. All of us can identify ourselves in the vignettes and dialogue. We are all variations of Ken, Pat, Bob, Jim, Kris, Jeff, and Carlos. I can't wait to start applying these principles to my own life. Tom Connellan has made the challenging simple and the simple challenging with his theories and guidance in this easy-to-read and easy to follow guide to improving one's performance and one's life."
Sandra King, Noted author and speaker on women and leadership

"Tom's books and teachings have played a big role in our ministry's progress. His other books are easy to read and profound in their impact. *The 1% Solution* is no different. Whatever your belief system, you will immediately benefit from reading this book because some of the tools work within 30 seconds and others within 30 days."
Reverend A. R. Bernard, Christian Cultural Center

"The ideas in *The 1% Solution* are simple, straightforward, and powerful. I've always known that little things make a big difference, and Tom not only proves the point in this excellent book, he also shows you how you can use *The 1% Solution* to get much better at what you do and how to help others get better, too."
Mark Sanborn, Author, *The Fred Factor* and *You Don't Need a Title to be a Leader*

"Making your life better can be daunting, but Tom Connellan shows in *The 1% Percent Solution* that you only need 1% percent improvement to get the ball rolling. This amazingly simple yet powerful concept can be applied to your career, personal relationships, finances, and much more. It's 160 pages of practical brilliance."
Susan M. Heim, Coauthor/editor, *Chicken Soup for the Soul* series

"Tom Connellan delivers on a big promise because *The 1% Solution* really does give you the magic formula for How to Make Your Next 30 Days the Best Ever. A wonderfully engaging business parable, *The 1% Solution* is full of timely insights and useful lessons that everyone needs to be reminded of from time to time. In a friendly format, author Tom Connellan captures life's eternal truths—just the sort of practical wisdom that Ronald Reagan and Ernest Shackleton used to coach themselves to extraordinary success."
Margot Morrell, Author, *Shackleton's Way—Leadership Lessons from the Great Antarctic Explorer* and *Reagan's Journey—Lessons from a Remarkable Career*

"Within an hour of starting *The 1% Solution*, I could feel the stress and pressure melting away because I knew I'd found my guide for making it through any challenge, including the tight economic times we're in right now. I shared Chapter One with my COO, and we have already started to think inside of the *1% Solution* model. A must-read and share for all entrepreneurs and business managers/owners!!"
Betsy Gordon, President, Equipment Locator Vendor Services

THE 1% SOLUTION

FOR WORK AND LIFE

HOW TO MAKE YOUR NEXT 30 DAYS THE BEST EVER

NEW YORK TIMES BESTSELLING AUTHOR

TOM CONNELLAN

THE 1% SOLUTION FOR WORK AND LIFE
HOW TO MAKE YOUR NEXT 30 DAYS THE BEST EVER

Printed in the United States of America.

Peak Performance Press, Inc.
1163 South Main Street, Suite 306
Chelsea, MI 48118
www.peakperformancepress.net

Distributed by National Book Network

FOR ADDITIONAL COPIES
VISIT YOUR FAVORITE BOOKSELLER

Quantity Discounts Available
CALL 800-945-3132
Visa/MasterCard/American Express/Discover

ISBN 978-0-9769506-2-2

Credits
Developmental editing: Vanessa Mickan
Interior design: Gwyn Kennedy Snider, GKS Creative
Cover design: Michele DeFilippo, 1106 Design

First Published 2011

CONTENTS

1

IT'S TURNING POINT TIME!

Ken powered down his computer at the end of the day and took a moment to sit back in his chair. It had been another productive day. Looking out into the hallway, he smiled and waved goodbye to one of his colleagues on her way out the door. It was great to have people around him that he could work with effectively. His eyes turned to the award he'd just had framed and hung on the wall, next to several others. He remembered how sweet it was to get each and every one of those awards—and the promotions and respect that went hand in hand with them.

And then he looked at his desk, at the pictures of his family. Ken had a great marriage, to a great woman. They loved each other and had a lot of fun together—and whenever life got tough, they had each other's back. As for his son and daughter, they were Ken's greatest pride and were always a joy to be around. Well, almost always—they were kids, after all, Ken chuckled to himself.

He took a satisfied, deep breath. He could honestly say he was a happy guy, that he was on top of the world.

But it hadn't always been this way . . .

Six months ago, Ken was in a slump. The smile fell from his face as he cast his mind back. He and his wife had seemed to be on a different page most of the time—bickering and finding faults with each other. The kids were butting heads and being defiant. They weren't doing so well in school, either. And Ken was on shaky ground at work. His job itself looked like it might be under threat, and every day he seemed to be in a battle with at least a couple of his colleagues.

He wasn't sure how he'd gotten into this slump. One day he'd just found himself there. He looked around at his friends, family, and colleagues, and realized that he actually had a fair bit of company. None of them seemed to know how they'd ended up there, either. Some didn't even seem to realize that they *were* there. So Ken wondered if this was just how life was meant to be.

Yet somewhere deep down, he still had a spark of hope that it was possible to achieve more, to *be* more. Suddenly the smile returned to Ken's face as he remembered his turning point.

§

It was a Saturday morning and Ken was watching his son Jake's first soccer game of the season. They were up against a team that had beaten them fairly consistently the previous year, so it wasn't as if he was expecting a great victory for Jake's team—but he always felt proud watching his son play. That day, though, he had to admit he was a little preoccupied and not quite as enthusiastic with his rooting as normal. He'd had the usual tough week and kept turning things over and over in his mind.

That was until partway through the game, when he realized that the encouraging shouts of the parents around him—"Good job!" "Nice work!"—were getting louder, more excited. The score was even; Jake's team was in control of the ball, within striking range of scoring.

The realization started to dawn on Ken that his son's team had had control of the ball a lot this game. Something had changed from last year. Jake's team was more focused and more responsive to the coach's instructions. They were playing more cohesively, more like a team. They were still kids—at times, they looked a bit like an amoeba going up and down the field, clustering around the ball—but no one could deny that they were sharper and playing better than they ever had before.

Jake's team was still made up of the same neighborhood kids he had been playing with for a few years. Sure, they were a year older, but so was the other team. Ken cast his eye over the other team, and saw that they were also pretty much the same boys as last year. The other team still had the same coach, too, standing on the opposite side of the field. Admittedly, he was wearing a puzzled expression that Ken had never seen on his face before, but it was definitely the same guy.

Ken couldn't remember Jake saying anything about a new coach for his team. He glanced away from the field for a second and saw that, sure enough, it was still Coach Jim sitting on the sidelines, where he always was.

Then Ken turned slowly to take a second look. It *was* Jim—but there was something different about him. Like the boys on the field, he seemed more switched on, more focused. There was something about his presence—the way he held himself displayed a certain self-confidence that hadn't been there before.

Then suddenly, Ken wasn't thinking about anything except the game. He was up on his feet, clapping and cheering along with the other parents, as Jake kicked the ball to one his teammates, who lined up and . . . scored.

Ken and the rest of the parents all gathered around at the end of the game congratulating Jake's team for their win, and praising the other team for their grit and effort. Amid the cheering and the high-fives, and the handing out of the end-of-game juice boxes and cookies, Ken caught Coach Jim's eye. He strode over and held out his hand so he could shake Jim's.

"Coach, congratulations, and thanks. My boy, Jake, has really improved out there on the field. So have all the boys. To be honest, the improvement is amazing," said Ken.

Coach Jim gave a small smile, and said, "The boys sure did a great job out there today. They practiced hard and gave it their all, and I'm very proud of them."

"I'm proud, too!" Ken said, turning now to Jake, who had just pulled himself away from his teammates for a second. Ken leaned down and gave him a great big hug, and said, "You did a great job out there, buddy!" before Jake raced back to continue celebrating with his teammates.

"What's your secret, Coach?"

"Ah," Jim said, "I had a feeling you were going to ask me something like that. I could see the cogs turning in your head."

"It's just that something's different this year. I don't know what you did exactly, but the team—they're *so* much better."

Jim said, "Thanks, they are doing better."

"It's not just that, though." Ken paused for a moment, and then looked the coach directly in the eye. "Look, I hope you don't mind me saying this, but it's not just the boys—*you* look different, too."

"I don't mind at all," said Jim, smiling broadly now. "Ken, you're right. I *am* a different man than I was at this time last year."

Jim turned and pointed to a bench beneath a tree a little ways from the crowd. "You got a moment to chat, Ken? I've been on kind of a journey since last season, and I think you're going to be interested in what I learned along the way."

Intrigued, Ken nodded and followed the coach, who stopped briefly to high-five one of the boys on his team and shake another parent's hand.

Once they'd moved away from the crowd and sat down, Jim said, "I was doing okay in my life. Not great, not terrible, just okay. But I had this nagging feeling that I could be doing more with my life.

"I've always gotten a great sense of achievement from coaching the kids, so I thought to myself, 'That's where I'll start. I'll help these kids become the best sportsmen they can be.'

"I figured that the first thing I needed to do was learn what raises the very best athletes above the rest. For me the ultimate test of excellence has to be the Olympics. Olympic athletes are so good that I personally can't tell the difference between any of the top competitors simply by watching them—can you?"

"Are you kidding! They line up at the start line, and seconds later, the race is over," Ken said.

"I remembered the excitement of being in front of the TV watching the men's downhill skiing at the 2006 Winter Olympics in Torino because it was so close," Jim went on. "So I went back and looked at the results. Ken, the difference between first place and fourth place— between a gold medal and *no* medal—was only 1.08 seconds, or *0.9 percent.*"

Ken whistled in amazement, and Coach Jim continued, "Well, that got me thinking. I began pulling up Olympic results from sports that come down to some objective measure of speed or distance or weight. I stayed up late calculating what separated the medal winners from the rest. Drove my wife nuts, of course— that is, until I showed her what I'd learned. She's a teacher, so she thought she knew everything there was to know about measuring excellence. Well, what I found out blew her away, too."

Ken raised his eyebrows and leaned forward in anticipation.

"Ken, whether it was swimming, track and field— you name it—the average difference between the gold medal winner and fourth place was just 1 percent.

"Sometimes it was a little more. In the men's 5,000-meter relay at the 2002 Winter Olympics in Salt Lake City, Canada won the gold with a time of 6 minutes, 51 seconds, while the U.S. came in at fourth place with a time of 7 minutes, 30 seconds—a difference of about 2.9 percent. But you know what? The teams that came in second, third, and fourth place had all fallen at some point in the race. Even with those falls, the difference between gold medal and no medal was only 2.9 percent.

"Sometimes, the difference was even less than 1 percent. In the men's 100-meter butterfly at the 2008 Beijing games, Michael Phelps was trailing—he was seventh out of eight swimmers—but in the last 50 meters, something remarkable happened: He managed to pass the five swimmers between him and the frontrunner, Serbia's Milorad Cavic."

Ken nodded, remembering the nail-biting finish.

"At the wall, it appeared that Cavic touched out Phelps. As Phelps finished, with a half-stroke, even he thought Cavic had won. But it turned out that the half-stroke had powered Phelps to the wall, in a time of 50.58 seconds, ahead of Cavic's 50.59."

"So wait a minute . . ." Ken worked it out in his head. "Phelps won gold by only 1/100 of a second?"

"Yep. You can't even blink that fast. There was only a 0.002 percent difference between gold and silver. And what separated a gold medal from no medal?" asked Jim. "Well, Phelps's margin of victory over the guy who came in fourth place was 0.15 seconds, or just one-third of a percent."

Ken thought of another example: "Did you happen to watch the women's 100-meter hurdles at Beijing? I'll never forget that race—to my eye, it was one big tie." "I studied that one, too," Jim replied. "You know what separated first place from seventh place? It was 18/100 of a second.

"Basically, the take-home message is: When you average it out, the difference between exceptional and *exceptionally* exceptional is 1 percent."

"One percent, that's really all it takes?" Ken asked. He felt that little spark inside him ignite for a moment. "That's incredibly powerful," he said. Then his gaze fell on the muddy, grass-stained neighborhood kids, and he had to swallow down a chuckle. "But Coach, really, you're not planning an Olympic campaign any time soon, are you?"

Jim didn't miss a beat. "Ken, you will never be an Olympian. I will never be an Olympian. These kids will probably never be Olympians. The real issue for those of us who aren't going to be Olympians—or the next Bill Gates, Wayne Gretzky, Oprah, Warren Buffett, Bobby Fischer, LeBron James, or Mozart—is this: 'What does that 1 percent mean for us?'

"I knew that no matter what I did, our team could never be 100 percent better than all the others. But 1 percent? We can all be 1 percent better at hundreds of things."

"You're really serious about this, aren't you?" said

Ken. He suddenly felt a bit naive for his flip comment about the coach's Olympic aspirations.

"Discovering the secret of The One Percent Solution opened up a whole world of new possibilities for me.

We can all be 1 percent better at hundreds of things. Think about it: I set out to train these kids to be 1 percent better in sportsmanship, teamwork, communication, perseverance, basic ball skills, and all kinds of life skills—and I think today's result proved that it worked. Imagine what The One Percent Solution can do for you, for me, for anyone who commits to improving, even by just 1 percent."

"I don't know, Coach. Seems to me it takes a whole lot of effort to get even 1 percent better at a few things, but at the end of the day, you still can't be guaranteed to come out on top," said Ken. "And we only remember the gold medal winners, don't we?" He sighed. "I don't know, sometimes it just seems like if you can't be the record breaker, there's no motivation to try harder."

"I've got another elite sporting example for you to think about, Ken," said Jim.

"I'll bet you have," said Ken, smiling.

"Okay, I'm going way back here, to 1990, to an Ironman event in New Zealand. You'd think that a 2.4-mile swim plus a 112-mile bike ride and a 26-mile run would separate competitors by at least several minutes, if not hours."

"Or in my case, perhaps even days," joked Ken.

"Well, only one second separated the winner, a Finnish runner, Pauli Kiuru, from the guy who came in second, American runner Ken Glah. What's really interesting here is that because of the spirit of competition, Glah still considers that second-place finish as one of the most glorious moments in his athletic career.

"My experience is that the journey and spirit of competition often overrule the notion of winning or losing. You may not win all the time, but you can have a winner's heart all the time if you're always trying to do something better today than you did it yesterday.

"It is my firm conviction that not everyone can be great, but everyone can be better than they are right now."

Jim gave Ken a moment to let that sink in, and then went on. "Do you remember the Olympic motto?" Ken shook his head, and the coach answered his own question: "It's *Citius, Altius, Fortius.*"

"Um, I'm a bit rusty on my Latin."

"Swifter, higher, stronger. Note that it does *not* say 'swiftest, highest, strongest.' It says 'swifter, higher, stronger.' That means working at getting better every day."

> Not everyone can be great, but everyone can be better than they are right now.

Ken stood up and started pacing in front of the bench—he was feeling too pumped up now to sit still. His mind was racing with all the ways that he could apply The One Percent Solution to his life. He stopped abruptly and turned to face Jim: "Does this solution apply to careers, too?"

"You bet it does. Maybe you're a sales rep or a marketing person or perhaps a manager—okay, you will never be 100 percent better than every other sales rep, marketing person, or manager. In fact, you'll just get discouraged trying to do that. But you *can* be 1 percent better at hundreds of aspects of the way you do your job. And as we've seen, 1 percent gives you an undeniable advantage."

"So you're saying this holds true for any career? Retail, IT, finance—"

"And for any aspect of your life you want to improve. I've seen people use it to improve their golf swing or their saxophone playing, to lose weight, to get fit . . . even to improve their family life." Recognizing a flash of recognition in Ken's eyes, the coach added quietly, "That's something that I think everyone can benefit from."

The soccer crowd was starting to thin out. Car doors were slamming in the parking lot, and the kids' yells were quieting down. "Come on, let's talk some more as we go back to our cars," Jim said.

As they set off, Ken asked, "Okay, so you worked out that you needed to help the team improve by 1 percent—but surely it's not that simple. How did you know where to start?"

"I was trying to figure out what I could do, how

I could get my arms around this. And then one day I was talking to a friend of mine. He's a top sales exec—if there were Olympics for selling, he'd be up there on the podium, let's put it that way. I told him about my theory and asked what I could learn from him, as he is so successful at what he does." Jim made a point of catching Ken's eye. "My friend said to me, 'Jim, it's time.'"

"It's time?" Ken looked quizzical.

"I'm going to tell you something that only a handful of people know, because I get the feeling that it's time for you, too.

"My friend introduced me to an incredible group of people who make it their life's work to achieve excellence. I was amazed when I met them, because it turned out that they were already living according to the principle I'd discovered in my research of Olympic results.

> I'm going to tell you something that only a handful of people know, because I get the feeling that it's time for you, too.

"They hadn't done the calculations showing that it's only 1 percent that separates the best performance from the rest, but they *had* worked out that it was just a slim margin. Their instincts and their experiences had already shown them that the way to success is through continually making small, targeted improvements.

"So when I came along and shared my data, for

them it was just like slotting the final piece of the puzzle in. Soon we had a name for our approach to creating excellence: The One Percent Solution.

"There are six of us now. Me, my friend the sales exec, a top physicist, a psychologist, a business owner, and this probably won't come as a surprise to you, a former Olympian.

"Don't worry, there are no meetings or secret handshakes—but you can think of us almost like a club. We take on people like you who are ready to make a shift in their life."

"Me?" said Ken, a bit startled. "Don't get me wrong, I'm grateful for the time you've just given me, but I never said . . ." His words trailed off as he realized that the coach had seen something in him that he was only just becoming aware of himself.

"If you are willing to make changes in your life, I will ask the others to share with you their secrets about achieving excellence. It won't be easy. You will have to leave behind some of your old habits, your old ways of doing things, and some of your beliefs about yourself and others. You can look forward to excitement and fulfillment, but I'm not going to sugarcoat it: There will be challenges along the way."

They were back at the group of kids and parents, which had thinned out by now. "Don't give me an answer now, Ken, but think about it," Jim said, then went to talk with another parent. Ken went to tell Jake and his best friend to jump in the car—the burgers were on him on the way home.

The kids were buckled in and Ken was just about to close the door when Jim appeared beside the car.

Ken looked up and said, "Thanks, Coach, you've really given me a lot to think about."

"You're welcome. I'm going to give you this." Jim handed him a business card. "Call me if you decide you're ready. Believe me, it's quite a trip."

2

THE UPSIDE-DOWN WAY TO BOOST YOUR MOTIVATION

Three weeks had passed since he'd received Coach Jim's business card, and Ken was sitting in his car feeling excited—and a little bit apprehensive—because he was about to meet the next One Percenter, the guy Jim said would win gold if there was such a thing as the sales Olympics.

It shouldn't have been a surprise that he was a busy man and Ken had to wait three weeks to see him. Ken would have gotten started sooner—in fact, he'd jumped on board the day after Jim handed him the business card. He had placed it on his bedside table the night after the soccer game and gone to sleep with the coach's words spinning around in his head, unsure of what to make of it all. But when he woke up—earlier than usual, as the sun was starting to rise—everything looked a lot clearer. He was certain that he was ready to make some changes. Become 1 percent better at various aspects of his life? He could do that.

In fact, he felt a deep *need* to do that.

§

The significance of his decision truly sank in when he picked up the business card and dialed Jim's number. The coach sounded pleased, but not surprised, to hear Ken's voice on the other end of the line.

"Welcome, Ken, it's great to have you aboard," he said. "But before we can get started, I need to tell you about three simple ground rules, and then you can decide if you can agree to abide by them." Ken thought there had to be some kind of catch.

"Number one: You can't tell anyone, except your wife, what you're doing," said Jim. "If people wonder what you've been up to outside of work, you can say something general, like you're having coaching or belong to a mastermind or mentoring group, but you must say nothing more. Can you agree to that, Ken?"

Maybe this wasn't going to be so tough after all, Ken thought. "Sure, I can agree to that, Coach."

"Number two: You may start this process only if *you commit to finishing the entire process.* We need your word that once you start, you will meet up with all six of the One Percenters and that you will apply what you learn to your life."

This rule was harder to commit to. Jim seemed to sense Ken's hesitation, and went on, "In return for your word, I can promise that you will succeed in reaching your goals. I can also promise that your success will radiate out from your initial intent and affect other areas of your life—your friends and family, your colleagues, your community."

"Jim, I've got to say, your confidence is inspiring, but can you really promise that?" Ken didn't want to sound skeptical, but before he agreed to something this big, he had to ask the questions that were on his mind. "What if I'm not up to it? What if it just doesn't work for me?"

"I can promise you this because I know that the concepts, tools, and techniques you are about to learn work. I can promise you this because these tools are not based upon opinion but upon solid research and testing, as you'll see should you choose to commit," said Jim.

> I can promise you this because these tools are not based upon opinion but upon solid research and testing, as you'll see should you choose to commit.

Ken was relieved to hear that Jim didn't sound at all offended by his questions. Jim wasn't pushing him, either. From the coach's voice, Ken suspected it was because his conviction was so deep that he didn't feel the need to push.

Jim continued: "I know you can do it because I've seen too many other people take these tools and do great things with them to believe otherwise."

Ken sucked in a deep breath, exhaled, and said, "Count me in."

"You're counted in," came the reply.

"But wait, what's the third rule?" asked Ken.

"Number three: Sometime within 180 days of completing the process, you must help at least one other person in the same way that you have been helped."

"So, within six months of meeting the last of the One Percenters, I have to share what I've learned with someone else?"

"That's right, Ken. Can you commit to that?"

Ken thought about the promising new kid who'd just been assigned to his team at work; he thought about the grown-ups that his son and daughter were going to become. If he could learn the keys to achieving excellence, it would be an honor to pass this knowledge on to others.

"When can I start?" he replied.

§

Jim had talked to the rest of the group, then called back to give Ken the phone number of the sales executive, Carlos. "You're gonna love him," Jim said. "He's the perfect guy to start out with; he'll really get you ramped up. His specialty is motivation." Then he added, "The man's a force of nature."

On the phone, Ken had been immediately impressed by Carlos's energy. He talked a mile a minute, and his excitement at starting Ken out with the basics of The One Percent Solution was infectious.

Carlos was on the road a lot for work, but they compared calendars until they found a few hours in their schedule to get together one evening.

"Do you like golf?" Carlos asked.

Actually, Ken struggled with golf. It wasn't so much that he didn't like it—more that it didn't seem to like him. He played occasionally because so much networking happened on the golf course—but he'd just never excelled at hitting that little white ball with a stick. And besides, didn't he and Carlos have *work* to do?

"Look, I'm not really a golf man, Carlos."

"Great! We'll meet at the driving range, then."

The guy mustn't have heard him right. But before Ken had a chance to set him straight, Carlos had moved on to the practical issue of how they would recognize each other.

"I'll be wearing a red baseball cap," Carlos said. "You wear one, too, and we can't miss each other."

"Uh, okay," agreed Ken.

"I'm psyched, Ken. Looking forward to it! See you then," Carlos signed off, rapid fire.

Ken knew it would probably have been easier to

search each other's names on the Internet for pictures, but now that he was sitting in the car and slipping the cap on his head, he was glad they were doing it this way. It made him feel ready. A touch nervous, but *ready*.

As he entered the driving range for the first time, disoriented for a moment by the floodlights and all the golf balls flying out toward the giant nets, he decided that Carlos hadn't really needed the red baseball cap after all. The range wasn't anywhere near full, and Ken recognized Carlos immediately: He had to be the human dynamo at the far end whacking balls faster and harder than just about anybody else, stopping only to pump his fist, accompanying the gesture with a silent "Yes!" when he was particularly happy with his effort.

Between shots, Carlos stopped to wipe his brow, and as he did, he noticed Ken. He put down his club and walked over with a brisk stride and a smile on his face. "Hi," he said confidently, stretching out his hand, "I'm Carlos, and you have to be Ken." The two men shook hands, and then Carlos turned abruptly and waved for Ken to follow. "Come on, let's get you started with some balls. You got your own clubs? Ah, that's right, not much of a golfing man." He laughed a good-natured laugh. "That's no problem, Ken. We're about the same size, so you can just use mine."

The two men began to hit, as they exchanged the basics—job, college, hometown, family. It turned out that Carlos was in charge of global sales for a major company that made golfing equipment—clubs, bags, balls, and the like.

Ken felt a bit stiff and awkward with his drives at first, pointing out to Carlos that it had been quite a few months since he'd played. Carlos waved away his concerns and in between his own hits offered some helpful suggestions. It seemed to give him a real buzz to be able to help Ken get even just a fraction better with his drives.

Ken started to feel the flow. Maybe he *could* see the appeal of this golf thing. There was certainly something satisfying about the club connecting with the ball with a thwack, especially when the ball sailed out in front of him a little straighter, a little farther, than when he'd started.

Plus, the comments such as "Nice shot" and "Way to go" coming from Carlos certainly helped his motivation.

Yet he was getting restless. Carlos was off on a round of conferences and conventions in a couple of days, and if they didn't get down to business soon, Ken wondered when they would have another chance.

His glance fell on his notebook, which lay open on a seat nearby. Coach Jim had told him so much at the soccer game that he'd asked him to go through it again over the phone so he could take notes. Well, not just notes—at the top, he'd written "To Do," to set his intention to follow through on what he'd learned. He planned to add to the to-do list every time he met with a One Percenter—though he probably didn't need to include pointers about his golf grip, he decided, smiling to himself.

Carlos followed his gaze and said, "I see you've been taking notes, Ken. That's good, that's good, taking it seriously. Good. So, what have you got for us? Fire away."

Ken read out:

"1. The difference between exceptional and EXCEPTIONALLY exceptional = 1 percent."

"Yep. Totally. What else you got?"

"2. You can't be 100 percent better than everyone else, but you can be 1 percent better at hundreds of things."

As Ken read out the next items on his list, Carlos murmured, "Yes," or "Keep going, I'm listening," all the time setting up balls and whacking them across the driving range.

"3. You may not win all the time, but you can have a winner's heart if you do something better today than you did it yesterday.

"4. Not everyone can be great, but everyone can be better than they are right now.

"5. Aim to be swifter, higher, stronger – not swiftest, highest, strongest."

Just as Ken was beginning to wonder whether Carlos was even listening, he turned to face Ken, flashed him a great big smile, and said, "You've got it all down perfectly! So what do you need me for?"

He wiped his hands on a towel, sat down, and gestured for Ken to sit, too. It was the stillest Ken had seen him so far. Carlos turned to face Ken and asked, "You agree that the points you've just read out are key to achieving excellence, right?"

"Yes. Yes, I do," Ken affirmed, though he was a little puzzled about where this was heading.

"Can you identify aspects of your life where you could make these 1 percent improvements?"

Ken paused for a second. He stared out across the driving range and thought about what he did at his job every day. Yes, he could definitely think of many things he could do a little better. Each on their own might not make an enormous difference, but combined, the improvement would be very impressive. Then he thought about the way he related to his wife and kids. Then about the way that he took care of his health and fitness. Again, he could think of many things he could start doing a little bit better right now.

Finally, he said, "Yes, I can think of many small improvements I could make every day that together could make a significant difference."

"Okay then, so why don't you just do them?"

Embarrassed, Ken bristled a bit at the question. He couldn't think of a good answer.

"Ken, what's stopping you from doing these things right now?"

"Honestly? I guess I don't really have any good reason," he said. He took off the red baseball cap and looked down at his feet, sounding a little defeated. "It's just that these days, I find that it seems hard to get motivated. And because I'm not motivated, I don't get much done."

"And then your motivation drops even further, because you're not getting much done?"

Ken looked up sharply then, and said, "Yes! Carlos, that's exactly right." He thought for a moment, slowly putting the cap back on, and added, "It seems to be affecting the people around me, too—the people who report to me at work, my family. If I can get more done, they'll be able to as well. I want to do the things that I know will help me improve, but I don't know how to get my motivation up to do them."

Ken thought Carlos must not have heard the quiet plea in his voice, because he was now doubled over laughing beside him. He was even slapping his thigh.

Ken thought he should probably be offended, but it seemed that everything this guy did was infectious, and pretty soon Ken's mouth was curling into a smile.

Carlos pulled himself together, sat up straight, and grabbed the notebook and pen out of Ken's hand.

"You're looking for a way to get your motivation up so you'll get more done. Right?"

Ken nodded.

"Okay, so let's diagram what you said this way." Carlos wrote:

"You're saying, if you were more motivated, you'd get more done. In other words, an increase in *motivation*"— Carlos pointed to the word and followed the arrow with his finger—"would lead to an increase in action."

"Exactly."

"And that's the only way?"

Ken stared at the sketch Carlos had made. It was pretty obvious to him that there was nothing else to it. He nodded.

"Now stand up, go over there, put a ball on the tee, and pick up the club you were using before."

Ken was so puzzled at this point that it seemed ridiculous to even argue or question him; he went over and did as Carlos said.

"Okay, so how did you feel about hitting a ball when

you first got here, Ken?" he said.

"Pretty crummy," Ken replied. "I was a bit uncomfortable, because I'm not exactly a natural at this."

"How do you feel about it now that you've done it a few times and achieved a little improvement?"

"Now? Well, I'm kind of looking forward to it. If nothing else, I'll release a bit of frustration on this ball," he said, grinning. He swung the club. And it was true, this time he actually *wanted* to do it.

When he sat back down, Carlos said, "Will you consider another possibility now? What if the arrow goes the other way, too?" Carlos drew another arrow on the diagram.

MOTIVATION ⟶ ACTION

"Maybe if you do more, your motivation will go up," said Carlos. "If you increase your *action*, your *motivation* will increase."

"Just like with the golf swing."

Carlos clapped his hands. "Just like with the golf swing!" Suddenly Ken could see why Jim had pegged Carlos as the motivation expert. His face was shining as he continued: "You see, Ken, you're absolutely right that motivation causes action. If you're motivated, you go out and do whatever it is you're motivated about. What too many people forget is that the reverse is at least equally true: *Motivation comes from having accomplished something.*

"What I'm suggesting is that the more you get done, the more motivated you are to do things. So you do more things, and you get even more motivated. It's a self-feeding cycle!"

Ken felt a surge of energy as he remembered a time when his greatest motivation came after he was able to accomplish something. "I remember learning to swim. Believe me, I was not motivated to learn to swim. Not at all, but we lived on the water, and my parents weren't taking no for an answer.

> The more you get done, the more motivated you are to do things. So you do more things, and you get even more motivated. It's a self-feeding cycle!

"So I took lessons. Not enthusiastically. Not even willingly, really. But I did take them. And once I learned some basic things—like the fact that I wasn't going to automatically drown—I kind of began to like it.

"I even asked my parents if I could take more lessons. I became good enough that I joined the swim team. Then I perfected my strokes. I've still got the trophies I won," he said, savoring the memories. "That's what you mean when you say that the best way to increase my motivation is to increase my action, isn't it?"

"Precisely!"

Ken was dumbstruck by the simplicity of it.

In fact, if it was this simple, why wasn't it already happening in his life, and everyone else's life? It was one thing for Carlos to say action leads to motivation—but look at him, Ken thought. He was such a high-energy, rock-'em-and-roll-'em kind of guy, motivation must never have been an issue for him. It seemed to burst out of him naturally, like water from a spring.

"But Carlos, aren't some people—you, for sure—just wired differently, to be more motivated than us mere mortals?"

"Ken, everyone can benefit from this, believe me." Carlos held Ken's gaze, and his voice was suddenly quieter as he went on, "When I was young and just starting out, I really didn't like public speaking. Tried to avoid it if I could."

"You?" Ken said. It was hard to imagine that the man who now made presentations to thousands of people a year could ever have felt that way.

"When a presentation had to be done at work, I'd just sit there praying someone else would volunteer. But one day, I decided to put my hand up to give a training session for a small group of new sales reps."

"How'd you do?" Ken asked.

"I aced it! No one else thought this training session was a big deal, but the sense of accomplishment I got from doing it successfully put me on top of the world.

That motivated me to volunteer for more presentations; I extended myself bit by bit, until now I don't have a problem with standing up in front of hundreds—thousands—of people.

"So you see, Ken, the real question is: Where do you start?

"The answer is that you start by doing something—however small—and once you accomplish that, your motivation goes up. And then you get more done. And then your motivation goes up. And then ..."

"You get more done ... and your motivation goes up," said Ken. "I'm liking where this is heading. Already I can see so many ways this can help me make 1-percent improvements."

> You start by doing something—however small—and once you accomplish that, your motivation goes up. And then you get more done. And then your motivation goes up. And then ...

Carlos high-fived Ken, and said, "There is one more key to this. I call it goal clarity. This is very important, so you might want to write it down: Be clear about what you want and *don't* want.

"If you put the motivation-action relationship into play, it is highly effective at increasing your motivation to do more—but if you use it to motivate yourself to perform tasks that don't contribute to your overall goal, you'll just be spinning your wheels."

"What you're saying is that before I choose my

actions, which will motivate me to do them even more, I need to be sure those actions contribute to my goal?"

"Yes! Let's say I want to be a better sales rep. I need to focus on actions like planning my sales calls better, choosing the right customers to call on, and finding out their needs—and not on actions like practicing my tennis serve.

"At the heart of this are two concepts that sound the same but are very different: The first is *effectiveness*, which is doing the right thing. The second is *efficiency*, which is doing things right.

"First, you have to make sure that what you're doing is the right thing—that you're being effective.

There's no point in doing well that which you should not be doing at all.

"Then, once you're sure you're doing the right thing, you have to be efficient at doing it, which means doing it really well. Sometimes, people get really good at doing things they ought not to be doing at all.

"Here's the headline on that: There's no point in doing well that which you should not be doing at all.

"Does that make sense?"

Ken said, "Uh-huh," as he wrote in his notebook.

"Then here's what I want you to do," Carlos said, which made Ken look up again. "Don't just take my word for it. Try it out and see it work in practice. Can you pick just one action you do that you know is the right thing to do and that you can do better? Remember, nothing big yet—this is just the beginning."

"Sure, I can pick one action."

"Can you do it tomorrow?"

Ken thought for a second. "Yes, I can do it tomorrow."

"And then the next day?"

Ken said, "Yes."

"Okay, how about for 30 days? That's all I'm asking for right now."

"For a month you want me to do one action that brings improvement? And you want me to start small?"

"You got it."

Ken was already thinking about the action he would begin to take tomorrow, and already looking forward to the whole new level of motivation it would bring to his life.

§

Ten days later, Ken had noticed an increase in his motivation.

He'd done his chosen action fairly consistently every day, although he had to admit it did feel strange to try something new.

He was downright surprised at how accomplishing the action made him feel more motivated to keep doing it.

Every so often, he'd pull out his notes and look at Carlos's diagram. And every time he looked at the

diagram, he was amazed at the simplicity and power of it. Starting with an action was simple and astonishingly effective.

He checked in with Carlos, who was his same bubbling self at first, then became very quiet and said, "You've made a good start—keep on doing things this way. Now you're ready for the next step."

3

THE PHYSICS OF PERSONAL SUCCESS:
HOW TO CREATE A MORE POWERFUL YOU

Ken was driving up a winding road in the hills just outside town, on his way to meet the next One Percenter. The farther he drove, the more trees there were, tall and green along either side of the road. The houses became farther and farther apart. He rolled down the windows to breathe in the refreshing, cooler air up here; it helped clear his mind and ready him for whatever his next teacher had to offer.

And this time, she was a teacher by profession—Pat, a college physics professor. She had sent him a link to her institute's website, and Ken was a little in awe of her even before they'd met. She had won all kinds of awards and made some pretty amazing breakthroughs. She even had a theory named after her. Now, as he pulled up in front of her home at the very top of a hill overlooking the city, he just hoped like crazy that she wouldn't spring a test on him at the end.

Pat opened the door with a big warm smile. Two Labradors came out, tails wagging; and as he walked in, he could smell the welcoming aroma of coffee. But he was a little taken aback at her appearance, and she sensed it straightaway.

"Not what you were expecting?" she said, still smiling.

"Sorry, uh . . . I, uh . . ." Ken had changed into jeans and a T-shirt after work, knowing that Pat was working from her home office that day. If he worked at home, he'd probably just wear jeans all the time. And Pat *was* wearing jeans, along with a casual T-shirt that wasn't tucked in. The strange thing was, she was also wearing a pair of very businesslike high-heeled shoes.

Pat laughed and led him through to the kitchen, her heels clicking on the tiled floor. "Ah yes, I'll explain later!" she said cheerily. Ken shrugged and chuckled along with her. If you were solving the mysteries of matter, time, and space, you could wear whatever fashion you liked, he guessed.

She poured him a coffee. Just like any good teacher, she was eager to find out what he'd learned from his previous session.

"Well, I felt like lack of motivation was holding me back from achieving things, but Carlos showed me that I could look at it the other way round," Ken said, and flipped open his notebook to show Pat the diagram Carlos had drawn.

MOTIVATION $\longrightarrow$ ACTION

She nodded her encouragement for him to continue, so he read out the key points on motivation and action:

1. The best way to increase motivation is to increase action.
2. The more I get done, the more I'll be motivated to do things.
3. The way to start is by taking action— even if it's a small action.
4. I need to be clear about my goals.
5. I must choose to do actions that help me achieve my goals (effectiveness), and then get good at them (efficiency).

A smile broke across Pat's face, but there was also a slightly faraway look in her eyes—Ken could see she'd had a "light bulb" moment. "Come this way, Ken!" she said. He followed Pat down the hallway, stopping along the way to be introduced to two of her kids, who were doing their homework.

Ken thought they were heading to Pat's office, so he was surprised to find himself in a big open playroom at the end of the hall. There were toys and gym equipment lying around, and an air hockey table.

"Played much air hockey, Ken?" Pat asked, though she already knew the answer from the look on his face.

"You could say that," Ken said. "Those are some lucky kids you've got." He couldn't resist picking up a paddle.

The puck was sitting in the middle of the table.

"Let's imagine for a second that that puck there is you," said Pat. "You're feeling unmotivated, can't get started on anything. You're stuck there, motionless."

"Okay," said Ken. He knew how that felt.

"What's going to happen to you, Ken?"

"Well, I guess I'll just end up sitting there like that indefinitely, not doing anything, not moving forward." His voice had sunk. "Unless . . ." He straightened up, leaned across the table, and knocked the puck with his paddle, setting it in motion.

"Yes!" Pat picked up a paddle and gave the puck a tap as it reached her end of the table. "Now you're moving!"

Pat turned on the air jets then, and the two of them started casually shuttling the puck back and forth. She asked Ken, "Would you be surprised if I told you that you just witnessed one of the fundamental laws of physics? Sir Isaac Newton's First Law of Motion, to be precise."

"Newton's first what?" said Ken. Knowing that she was at the top of her field, he'd assumed she was going to share her tips for becoming one of the elite—but actual *physics*?

"A key part of The One Percent Solution is this law of motion, first discovered by Newton," Pat said. Checking to make sure she had Ken's full attention, she went on and told him the law:

"*Unless acted upon by an outside force, a body at rest stays at rest and a body in motion stays in motion.*"

"Let me get this straight. Unless some force acts on it, if the puck's resting it will stay resting and if it's moving, it will stay moving." Pat nodded, and Ken had his own "light bulb" moment.

"That's why I sometimes go through a period when I don't seem to get much done—until something happens and it gets me going," he said.

"Exactly, Ken. You might be stuck in a familiar rut, but then along comes some outside circumstance—it might be a change in the economy, an illness, a change in your family life. Whatever the force is, it makes you act—just as when you hit the hockey puck you put it in motion."

Ken was focused on the implications of this principle, and while he was thinking, Pat shot the puck right into the goal slot directly in front of him. He picked it up, put it back in play, and said, "When I wait for a circumstance to get me moving, I hardly ever end up doing what I really want to do, but what I *have* to do just to get by."

"Well, here's where it gets good, Ken. Because you are not just an inanimate hockey puck, but rather a human being with a will, you don't *have* to sit around waiting for circumstances to force you to act.

"You can do what Carlos suggested: start to do one action to improve an area of your life that matters to you. And because Newton's law works, once you get yourself in motion, you'll stay in motion."

Because Newton's law works, once you get yourself in motion, you'll stay in motion.

"But wait a second, if that was really true, how did the puck end up sitting on the table motionless?" asked Ken. "If something that's in motion stays in motion, the puck should have still been bouncing all around the table from the last time someone played."

"So, Ken, when are you enrolling in one of my courses?" Pat replied, her eyes sparkling. Ken was the kind of student who made teaching fun.

She switched off the air jets and sent the puck very gently down the table by hand. They watched as the puck slowed, until it stopped in the middle of the table. Ken looked across at Pat a little triumphantly, as if to say, "See!"

"Friction, Ken," the professor finally said. "The air jets made the friction less apparent. Now I've turned them off, we can see that there *is* in fact a force acting on the puck."

"It's just that it's an *unseen* force," said Ken, slowly, "and even with air jets, there's still some small amount of friction, so if you stop hitting it, eventually the puck comes to a stop."

"That's right," she answered. "And once a force brings something to a stop, Newton tells us that *inertia* keeps it there. Inertia is the enemy of anyone who strives for excellence, because it keeps you motionless, at rest, not moving forward. That's why starting with the action part of the motivation-action equation is so important."

"Because just by putting one foot in front of the other, I'll put myself into motion," said Ken, fully grasping it now.

"Yes," Pat agreed, and then added, "Once you get in motion, you've overcome that initial inertia that was holding you in place. At that point, the momentum you've built keeps you moving ahead. And as long as you're facing in the right direction, you'll be making progress."

"Unless an outside force stops me," said Ken.

"Yes, those outside circumstances again. Sometimes you don't have control over those," Pat said, "but by returning each time to this law, you can always put yourself back in motion and working toward your goal of 1-percent improvement every day."

Pat turned the air jets on again, raised her paddle, and grinned. "Time for a break, don't you think?"

§

When Pat's kids had finished their homework, they came to lay claim to the air hockey paddles, and Ken followed Pat to her office to continue their discussion. The walls were mostly glass, and sitting opposite Pat at her desk, Ken felt as if they were surrounded by nothing but tall green trees and a big blue sky.

"I feel as though the possibilities are enormous for the improvements I can achieve," he said. "But Carlos stressed that I should choose only one small action. I know I've just started, but I haven't noticed my wife and kids and coworkers being appreciative—actually, they've looked at me a bit like I'm from another planet.

"I've got to wonder what kind of an improvement I can expect if I make only a small change. Is it really going to be significant?"

"Yes, Ken, it is. I know this for a fact," said Pat with certainty. "Let me tell you a story. When my institute decided to allow more telecommuting, I jumped at the chance to set up a home office. It sounded ideal because I had a one-hour commute each way that was driving me nuts. Working a few days a week at home would mean fewer distractions, and I would be more productive.

"Well, it didn't quite work out that way—at least not at first. I started finding all sorts of chores around the house to do and errands to run. I started putting work tasks off, thinking I could do them in the evening if I needed to.

"I ended my weeks having completed only half of what I needed to get done. And then I'd pull all-nighters. I was acting like my students when they have a paper to hand in to me!" A sad look passed over her face as she said, "To be honest, it was causing a lot of stress.

"The turnaround came in the form of these," she said, swinging her feet out to the side and clicking her heels together. "My sister gave these shoes to me and said they were my work shoes, and that putting them on meant I was starting work and taking them off meant I was finishing for the day. They have done wonders. I can't in good conscience do something other than work when I'm wearing them. Now it's only my students who are pulling the all-nighters, and my productivity *is* greater than when I was commuting to the office all the time."

"I guess you could say that was a small change in action leading to a big result!" said Ken. "You know, that reminds me of my cousin who runs a bakery and coffee shop. His storefront had no windows and a deep entrance, and he wasn't allowed to put a sidewalk sign out. People simply weren't noticing his place. Then one day, he had a stroke of genius. He set up a small table just outside the door and a little to the side. On the table he put some freshly made baked goods. And a fan.

"People stopped and looked around until they'd figured out where the smell was coming from. His sales doubled in one week! He had the table in his garage, and the fan cost $12. He talks about it as one of those fluke things, just good luck, but is this the kind of small change you're saying we should be on the lookout for?"

"Yes, Ken. In fact, it's a great example of leverage, the next law of physics I want to tell you about," Pat said, leaning forward eagerly. "Leverage unlocks the power of a small change in behavior. You can make a small change and see outsized improvement."

"Newton again?" asked Ken, leaning forward and eager, too.

"No, we have to go farther back this time, to the ancient Greek Archimedes."

Pat cleared some papers off the desk, lay a pencil down, and balanced a ruler on top of it. Then she picked up a big hardcover dictionary from the bookshelf beside her and plunked it in front of Ken. "Okay, pick that book up off the desk with one finger."

He could lift it partway off the table with one finger, but it wasn't easy.

She took the book from his hand and placed it on

one end of the ruler. "Now try pushing on the other end of the ruler—the lever—with one finger."

With very little effort on Ken's part, the book rose completely off the table.

"Archimedes put it something like this: 'Give me a lever long enough and strong enough; give me a fulcrum; give me a place to stand—and I will move the world.' Compelling stuff, huh?"

"I will move the world," Ken repeated, pressing down and lifting the book a few more times.

I will move the world.

"The right small shift in what you do leads to outsized results compared to the effort you put in. People at the top of any field are very good at identifying and using opportunities for high-leverage actions," Pat said.

"So it's really about picking the right small change to the way you do things," chipped in Ken. "I mean, putting on a certain pair of shoes isn't a big effort, nor is what my cousin did. But the results are so much greater than the effort."

"That's right, Ken. It's the 20/80 Principle. You may have heard of it—it's sometimes called the Pareto Principle."

Ken nodded; he'd come across it in training sessions at a few companies he'd worked for. She'd muddled it up and called it the 20/80 Principle instead of 80/20, but that was understandable—it was getting late in the day.

"It all started with the economist Pareto, who noticed that 20 percent of the people own 80 percent of the wealth," she said. "And it turns out that this relationship can be seen everywhere. On average, 20 percent of a company's products account for 80 percent of their revenue; for restaurants, it's 20 percent of the items on their menu that bring in 80 percent of their revenue. In my work, I know that about 20 percent of my students need about 80 percent of my time. You probably can see the 20/80 Principle at work every day, too."

Ken thought about all the 20/80 splits he could see in his own job.

Then he said, "Pat, I can certainly see this in practice in all aspects of my life—but just so you know, it's actually called the 80/20 Principle." He didn't want someone this smart to embarrass herself by using the term the wrong way in front of other people. "And usually it's applied to *things*—like the 80 percent of a company's products making up 20 percent of its sales that you just mentioned. But I thought we were talking about changing the way we *do* things."

"Hah, yes! Seriously, when are you signing up for one of my classes?" She jumped up from behind the desk and rolled a big whiteboard over. She had obviously been working out a problem on one side—it was covered in what looked like hieroglyphics to Ken—and she flipped it over to the other side, which was clean.

"Our behavior—our actions, if you like—lead to certain results." She drew:

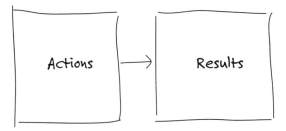

"The 20/80 Principle also applies to this relationship. It goes beyond external factors like customers and products in a warehouse. It relates directly to you, Ken. To everyone. It relates directly to you, your actions, and the results those actions produce.

> Because of the power of leverage, a relatively small change in the way we do things can have an outsized effect on the results we achieve.

"Because of the power of leverage, we know that a relatively small change in the way we do things can have an outsized effect on the results we achieve. Right?"

"Yes," Ken said, and then Pat added to the diagram:

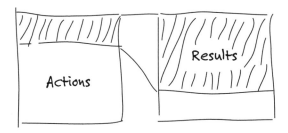

"As you can see, what you need to focus on are the behaviors that produce the outsized results, rather than the results themselves. You need to identify and start doing actions like those that produce the outsized results," Pat said. "That's why I call it the 20/80 Principle."

She completed the diagram by giving it a heading:

20/80 Principle

"Calling it the 20/80 Principle brings attention to what we really need to focus on: *We need to focus on small shifts in our actions that will produce large shifts in our results.*"

"The 20/80 Principle," said Ken, trying it out. He liked the sound of it and the way it really did put the focus where it needed to be. "Even with that common example in which 20 percent of a company's products account for 80 percent of the revenue, I can see that it's more helpful to think of it as the 20/80 Principle. Rather than thinking first of the 80 percent of the revenue, it is more useful to look first at the 20 percent of the products that are producing 80 percent of the revenue."

He imagined the kind of improved results companies could see if they focused on the characteristics of that 20 percent of products, the types of customers who bought them, similar new products on the market, and so on. Then Ken smiled to himself, realizing that the act of changing the focus from 80/20 to 20/80 was itself an example of a slight change in action that could produce outsized results, because it helped you focus on small shifts in action that could produce large shifts in accomplishment.

"You should see what Carlos did in his company with his understanding of leverage," said Pat. "He explained the ideas behind The One Percent Solution to everyone in the company and asked them all to commit to improve something by 1 percent."

"I think that's just brilliant," said Ken. "I mean, who could possibly say no to making a 1-percent improvement?"

"Exactly. And then he spent a lot of time with all the people who directly report to him and identified small changes in behavior that would bring outsized results.

"One of the things they did sounds so simple. They made sure that everyone started treating their colleagues in a more respectful and positive manner, because it turns out that you end up treating customers the same way you treat one another.

"Then he went to the sales department and worked

with his three sales managers to identify a couple of high-leverage changes in the way the sales reps did their jobs. The changes weren't such a big deal for the reps to make, but they would produce outsized improvements to the company's bottom line.

"Carlos says the results were amazing. The changes might have been relatively small, but they were high-leverage changes, and his company is even more profitable now.

"And he came to me a few months later and shared an exciting discovery," she added. "There was a side effect to the changes—a wonderful side effect.

"When you drop a stone in the middle of pond, the ripples spread out and affect the whole pond. The same with The One Percent Solution. Once you get started making the right changes to how you do things, the impact radiates out and affects all the relationships around the initial point of entry."

"Really?" asked Ken. "In what way?"

"In Carlos's case, soon *everyone* in the company was more fully engaged in their jobs. They were even going to their managers to make further suggestions for changes that could bring outsized results."

"So, what was happening was that certain people at the company had made some small but well-targeted changes to their behavior that resulted in improvements," Ken said, to make sure he was understanding correctly. "It didn't matter that what they did was only a 1-percent change, because it was the kind of change that produced outsized results. And the ripples spread throughout the company."

"That's right, Ken. Once people saw results, they became motivated to try other new things. When those worked, they kept doing more. That's a real-life example of momentum building, by the way. It's back to that motivation-action diagram, see?" Pat said, leaning across to flick back through Ken's notebook. She picked up the pencil and said, "May I add something?"

"Of course," said Ken.

Pat wrote a heading so that it now read:

Ken looked out over the treetops and thought for a moment about how the right high-leverage changes might affect his workplace. He imagined what it would be like when the impact rippled through the whole workplace, and when the motivation-action cycle led to everyone feeling a greater engagement with their jobs. He envisioned how momentum would help keep the whole process going.

After giving him a moment to absorb everything, Pat went on, "Now, I don't want to give you the impression that this is something that's just for big corporations, Ken. I'm always telling my students that the laws of physics apply to everything we can see around us—and plenty of things we can't see, too! Well, I'm going to say the same thing to you.

"These principles apply to any aspect of your life. They apply to career, personal health, fitness, and learning a new skill or honing one," she said.

"How about relationships?" asked Ken.

"The One Percent Solution has been really important in my personal life," Pat answered. "When Carlos told me about his results and I saw how using leverage and momentum together in the right way can crystallize into engagement, I realized something I wasn't proud of," she said quietly.

The One Percent Solution has been really important in my personal life.

Ken quickly turned from the window to look at her.

"I wasn't fully engaged in my marriage. I wasn't fully engaged with my kids. I wasn't fully present."

Ken was nodding now, a friendly signal to let her know she certainly wasn't alone.

"Oh, the scientist in me isn't used to talking about stuff like this, but, well, I started off with really small things. They sound kind of goofy now . . ."

"Please, Pat, go on. I bet they're a lot less goofy than you think, and very helpful."

"Okay, well, first I decided that when my family spoke to me, I'd aim to be less distracted. I'd pay close attention while I was listening, by focusing on their eyes.

"Each day I would do one thing that showed I loved them—a hug, a cuddle, or saying 'I love you.'

"Once a week, I would do something special, like cook their favorite meal or do one of their chores for them."

Ken turned away again, his eyes slightly moist. "Pat, those are great things to do," he said. A line from a song by one of his favorite groups popped into his mind: "A kind word never goes unheard but too often goes unsaid." It was time to start saying some of those words, he thought. In fact, the actions Pat had mentioned were all easy things he could start doing right away that would have an outsized impact.

"The ripple effect came into play here at home, too—although not straightaway," said Pat. She laughed and went on, "I know what you mean about being looked at like you're from another planet. But before long, the impact spread out to not just my kids and husband, but to my friends and family, too. Pretty soon, *I* was receiving more hugs, having my favorite meal cooked for me now and then, and I was noticing that people were giving me their fullest attention when I spoke."

"And you're sure it wasn't just wishful thinking?"

"Oh, yes. There's scientific evidence to back this up,"

she replied, and Ken noticed how much more at ease she sounded talking about facts again.

"If you have an obese friend, you are 57 percent more likely to be overweight," she said. "If you're a smoker and you have a friend who quits, you are 30 percent more likely to be successful than if your friends smoke.

"But here's the really interesting research." She opened one of her desk drawers and pulled out a piece of paper. Ken noticed that it said "*Connected*, by Nicholas Christakis and James Fowler" at the top.

"These are my notes on a book a couple of professors from Harvard and UCLA wrote about a long-running study they did. They found that when you become happier, it can have such a profound ripple effect that you can make people happier who you don't even *know*."

"Are you kidding?"

"This is for real. If you're happy"—she began reading from her notes—"your next-door neighbor is 34 percent more likely to be happy.

"Your spouse is 8 percent more likely to be happy.

"Your brother or sister living within a mile is 14 percent more likely to be happy.

"Your friend living within a mile is 25 percent more likely to be happy.

"Your friend's friend is 10 percent more likely to be happy."

"Wow, even your *friend's* friend," Ken interjected.

"Wait, you'll love this: A friend of a friend of your

friend is 5.6 percent more likely to be happy.

"Naturally, it doesn't just flow in one direction. So if your next-door neighbor becomes happy, that naturally increases by 34 percent the probability that you and your family will be happy."

Ken looked astounded and joyful all at once. "It's not just Archimedes. Each of us really does have the power to move the world, don't we?"

"One percent at a time!" Pat added.

Each of us really does have the power to move the world 1 percent at a time!

4

WHY PRACTICE DOESN'T MAKE PERFECT, AND WHAT TO DO ABOUT IT

Coach Jim had been right when he said this would be quite a trip, thought Ken. He could hardly believe the amazing places he was going and people he was meeting now that he'd committed himself to the path of achieving excellence. It was casual Friday, and he had felt pretty darn good seeing the reaction of people in the office when he told them why he'd dug his boating shoes out from the bottom of the closet and was wearing shorts: He was going sailing after work. It was tempting to break the ground rules, but he managed not to drop the name of the man whose boat he would be sailing on—a respected business owner who cropped up in the business news headlines from time to time.

Before he got up from his desk at the end of the day, Ken took a moment to go over what he'd learned from Pat about the laws of momentum and leverage that underlie The One Percent Solution—he figured the deck of a boat was no place for his notebook. His to-do list read:

1. Taking action overcomes the inertia holding you in place.
2. Momentum keeps you in motion.
3. The right leverage brings outsized results compared to the effort you put in.
4. Because of the 20/80 Principle, you should look for small shifts in your actions that can lead to large shifts in your results.

20/80 Principle

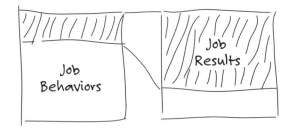

5. Momentum, leverage, and the ripple effect lead to engagement.

ENGAGEMENT!

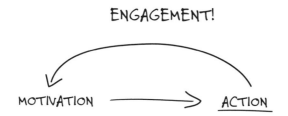

MOTIVATION $\longrightarrow$ <u>ACTION</u>

Though he had to admit to the occasional day of slacking off, for the past couple of weeks, he had been mostly keeping up with the small changes he had chosen to make at work and at home. A couple of times, he even thought he might be starting to see a little of the ripple effect Pat had talked about.

As he flipped over to a clean blank page, which he would fill after his next learning session, he felt a buzz of excitement.

§

Bob clearly wasn't one for chit-chat. As they made their way out of the dock, between the other boats moored in the harbor, he said little to Ken but the necessary instructions. The businessman and sailor had a quiet confidence about him, Ken thought. And he bet that when Bob had something to say, people sure as heck listened.

Once they had made their way clear of land and other boats, they hoisted the sails. For a moment, they sat there in friendly silence, eyes on the expanse of sea and sky in front of them as the boat knifed through the water.

Then Bob pointed and said to Ken, "We're heading for that." It was a small island—more of a rocky outcrop. Ken's palms got a bit sweaty when he realized a good strong wind was blowing from that exact direction. "You remember how to tack?" Bob asked.

Ken nodded, though a little uncertainly. He knew that when you were facing into the wind, you had to maneuver to allow the wind to fill the sail first on one side, then on the other, so that you zigzagged to your destination. He was a little rusty, but it should come back to him.

Bob put Ken through his paces a few times, heading the boat first one way, then after a while, tacking back in the other direction but always maintaining about a 40-degree angle to the island. Then he began to step up the pace, changing tack more quickly each time. Jumping up to switch from one side of the boat to the other as Bob steered the boat through its turns, Ken felt as if he was back at high school football practice going through two-a-day drills. He had to focus hard to keep up, not just hopping from one side to the other, but also loosening the lines holding the jib—he seemed to remember that's what the smaller sail on the front was called—and then hauling them on the opposite side, while Bob trimmed the mainsail.

After giving him a moment to mop the sweat from

his brow, Bob handed Ken control of the tiller and said, "In your own time." Ken's mouth was dry and salt water was lashing his face as he began to turn the boat across the wind—was it his imagination, or did it suddenly seem to have strengthened?

After maintaining the same course for a short while, Ken decided to tack. He pushed the tiller over carefully—a little too carefully and not quite far enough, apparently, because the momentum the boat needed to complete the turn was lost. The wind hit them head on. Ken was amazed that he had the clarity at this moment to think of Pat and what she'd said about a body in motion remaining in motion unless it was acted upon by an outside force . . .

The sails never filled but merely flapped back and forth, and the boat stalled—and then to Ken's embarrassment, it seemed to be pushed backward by the wind. Bob never flinched and simply had him hold the tiller all the way over until the boat stopped being pushed backward and got headed slightly off in one direction. Soon, the wind was filling the sails and they were back on course.

"In sailing, this is one of the most fundamental skills you need to master—paying attention to the conditions around you and adapting in response, so that you are always moving forward," Bob said. After a pause, he added, "Just like in life."

Pointing to the rocky island, he continued: "Say

that's your goal. You need to understand that if all you're meeting is resistance, maybe you need to approach your goal from a slightly different angle. Know your goal, then focus on the right course that leads you to it.

"That means no falling asleep at the wheel, Ken."

"Yes, sir," he answered.

"Imagine if you *did* let your focus stray from your course and your goal," said Bob. "Imagine if you let it stray by just 1 percent."

"I might sail past the island, it's fairly small."

"That's right, Ken. And you'd have to waste time getting back to it. Or you might even crash into the reef that's beneath the waves just to the west," answered Bob. "Of course, you wouldn't miss the island by much, because it's a relatively close goal, right?"

"Sure."

"But let's say it's a longer-term goal. Let's say I ask you to sail us to England."

"Let me make a few calls—I've got a few things I'll need to clear from my schedule," said Ken, laughing.

Bob smiled and said, "Yep, we'd sure have a big expanse of ocean to cover—probably take us 30 to 40 days if the conditions were good. If, on average, you were off by just 1 percent, over that distance—assuming you could take the shortest route without tacking, which of course you couldn't—you'd end up in either France or Ireland, depending on whether you were off 1 percent to the starboard or 1 percent to the port."

"And that's a just goal maybe 40 days in the future and only 1 percent off target. Some of my goals are *much* more distant than that, and I could drift much farther off course," said Ken. He thought about where he wanted to be in five years' time, and by the time his kids were ready for college, and by the time he was ready to retire . . .

"One percent counts, Ken. It counts."

Bob had that undeniable aura of a leader, Ken thought. His white hair was in a crew cut, and he had the build and the leathery skin of a born and bred sailor.

"Bob, is there a secret to how you got to be so good at sailing? You just look like such a natural."

"You kidding?" said Bob. "Where I was born, it was all farms. We hardly saw swimming pools, let alone the ocean. Then when I was a teenager, my cousin moved to a lake and bought himself a sailboat. Every summer I went to stay, and pretty soon, I was hooked on sailing.

"But I was no natural. I had my share of near misses with the dock or the boom. I tipped over. I ran aground. I practiced, though. I joined a beginners' sailing class filled with kids who were five, six years younger than me. I drilled before and after the class. I put in hour after hour after hour of practice, until I was competition standard and eventually had my own boat that I raced. We—it took six to race it—would drill during the week and debrief during and after the race."

Bob paused to draw all of Ken's attention before he said, "That's a crucial thing you need to know about

The One Percent Solution. There is no such thing as 'a natural.'

"Forget all that stuff about these successes who just happen to have a natural talent for something. That's bull. It's all about practice." Bob then asked Ken, "Is there something you want to be really good at?"

"Sure," said Ken. He didn't care so much about being a great sailor, but when he thought of his career, relationships, family life, and health and fitness, there were plenty of things he wanted to be really good at.

"Well, I don't care what anyone else says, if you want to get good at something, it's all about practice. Practice, practice, practice. In fact, to be the best of the best, you'd have to practice for 10,000 hours."

Ken looked back at the captain blankly. Where had he plucked that figure from?

"It's been proven in a few different studies," Bob continued. "If you want to make it to the elite level of anything—business, math, science, music, literature, chess, pinochle, whatever—it takes 10,000 hours of deliberate practice."

"But that's such a long time. Even if you practiced 20 hours a week—well, that's 10 *years*."

"Uh-huh."

"What about people who were just born with an incredible talent? Like . . . like a brilliant concert pianist?"

"My granddaughter actually *is* a top classical musician, Ken. A violin soloist. I've seen the hours she puts in. Someone's even studied how much time people like her spend practicing: A psychologist named Anders Ericsson got together with some other experts and studied violinists at an elite music school. Divided them up into the ones who were bound to be stars, the ones who were really good and could play professionally, and the ones who were good but not *great* and who'd probably become violin teachers.

"The only difference they could find? The number of hours of practice the musicians put in. The ones who were good enough to teach—they'd put in 4,000 hours. The ones who were really good and could play professionally—8,000 hours. The cream of the crop, the brilliant soloists?" he said, looking to Ken for the answer.

"Let me guess . . . 10,000 hours." The two men shared a smile.

"The scientists couldn't find one single natural— someone who got to the top without all that practicing because they were just brilliant," added Bob. "And you know what's great? They didn't find any sad old grunts who were practicing their hearts out but not getting anywhere.

"The take-home message here is: If you put in the time and effort to practice, you *will* see improvement. And if you want to see improvement, you have to put in the practice."

"Bob, I can't help but wonder, is it the same in

business? Some people just seem to have an instinct for making the right move. I mean, look what Bill Gates did that no else could come close to achieving."

"Okay, let's look at Bill Gates," replied Bob. "Malcolm Gladwell wrote about him in his book *Outliers*. He talked about how at high school, Bill skipped gym and snuck out in the middle of the night to go steal time on a university's computers so he could learn programming. His parents always wondered why it was so hard to wake him up in the morning! But by the time he was a Harvard dropout, he'd put in way more than 10,000 hours of practice at programming. He'd done more practice than just about anyone else on the planet."

Ken didn't look entirely convinced. Surely some people were just born to be great. "What about the very top sportspeople? I mean, just look at Wayne Gretzky. That guy could see stuff no one else could. I remember he'd be flying down the ice full speed and pass the puck *backward* to a teammate he couldn't possibly have seen." Ken shook his head in amazement, recalling the plays he'd rewound and watched over and over, trying to work out how Gretzky pulled off his magic tricks. "Even *he* couldn't explain it! He said he had a 'feeling' for where other players were on the ice and could just pass without even looking. He didn't go to where the puck *was*; he went to where the puck was *going to be*."

"It might look like he had a sixth sense, but sports

scientists who study these things say that in fact his brain just processed all the cues around him better than anyone else's did," said Bob. "Think about it. How many hours of practice and playing do you think he put in, starting with the thousands of hours he spent with other kids on the homemade rink behind his family's house? And then thousands of hours with his teammates.

"I know a former college player who noticed that the sound of his opponents' skates on the ice changed when they were about to make a move. That knowledge gave him a slight time advantage over others in countering their move. If my friend could do that, consider the possibility that Gretzky could tell exactly where to pass just from the sound of skates hitting the ice behind him—all without even consciously thinking about it.

"Scientists have even worked out video-game-type training to help hockey players develop that field sense like Gretzy's. They train them to better process the information around them. If practice could help you develop a skill like that, which seems out of this world, think of all the other skills you could develop if you practiced."

Ken thought about how he could use this knowledge in the future and benefit from it. Then he said, "Boom over!" With Bob's help, he was beginning to feel a little more comfortable maneuvering the boat. But he fell silent as he stared at the small rocky island they were getting close to.

He was doing math in his head, and it confirmed what he thought: He'd put in way more than 10,000 hours at work, but he still felt as though he hadn't achieved mastery in his career. He'd reached a plateau that he couldn't seem to step up from.

And he had put in more than 10,000 hours at maintaining relationships and being a parent. So why was it still a struggle some days?

"Bob, I put in 45 to 50 hours a week at my job. That's at least 2,200 hours a year, and I've been there five years, which is at least 11,000 hours. So shouldn't I have been made CEO a while back? And what about people I see who have 30 to 40 years of experience but just aren't all that sharp in their job?" Though all of this bugged him, Ken tried to inject a light, joking tone into his voice.

Bob replied, his tone 100 percent serious, "Let me answer your second question first. Too many people who have been around for 30 years don't really have 30 years' experience. They have one year's experience 30 times. They've never grown.

Too many people who have been around for 30 years don't really have 30 years' experience. They have one year's experience 30 times.

"Now, back to your first question: You're wondering why you haven't reached the top if you've already put in more than 10,000 hours? Well, it's more than just the *quantity* of hours of practice. It's also about the *quality* of those hours. That guy I was telling you about, Anders Ericsson, he calls it *deliberate practice.*

"Deliberate practice is designed specifically to improve performance. It is able to be repeated. It comes with constructive feedback," said Bob, as if he was checking off bullet points. "And it's not about fun. It's difficult. Sometimes it's very difficult work."

"Well, I'd hardly call my work 'fun,'" replied Ken, a little defensively. He'd stopped trying for a light tone.

Bob raised a conciliatory hand and said, "Ken, I don't doubt the effort and hard work you put into your career. Really, I don't.

"But let's say being the very best in the country at what you do is your goal and you feel you're not making progress. There are a few questions you need to ask yourself."

Ken nodded once. "Shoot."

"Did you ever play a musical instrument when you were young, Ken?"

"Yup. Piano."

"How much time did you spend practicing each day?"

"Thirty minutes Tuesday through Friday, and a lesson every Monday."

"How much time did you spend *deliberately* practicing a day?"

Ken thought back to those afternoons at the piano, sneaking glances out the window and wishing he was out playing ball with the other kids. "Honestly? None . . . or 30 minutes each Monday if you count the lesson."

"Now let's jump ahead a few years."

"I don't think I like where this is going." Ken smiled, in a gritted-teeth kind of way.

"Probably not. But I think you'll like where it takes you," replied Bob. "Not counting the hours you spend on admin tasks and reporting and other stuff that doesn't involve your specific job skills, how much time a week do you spend performing those skills?"

Ken whistled in surprise after he'd thought about it. "Maybe 18 or 20 hours."

"How much time to you spend *deliberately practicing* your job skills?"

There always seemed to be so many distractions at work—Ken cut himself off from that train of thought, because he was only making excuses. Truly, he almost never went out of his way to do things at work that were specifically designed to improve his performance, could be repeated, involved getting constructive feedback, and were challenging. He shook his head. "Maybe an hour a month."

"That's because, like most people, you're *performing* tasks, not *deliberately practicing* them."

Ken felt for a second as though he'd been sleep-walking and Bob had just shaken him awake.

"Maybe even more importantly when it comes to achieving your career goals, how much time do you spend *deliberately* practicing the skills of the *next* job you want to have?"

Silence from Ken for a moment, then, "Well, if we're talking CEO, I guess that would mean leadership skills, strategizing, coming up with the big-picture vision . . ." He trailed off, realizing that he focused all his attention on the job at hand and rarely thought about developing skills for the future. In fact, he spent little time in *deliberate* practice at any of the things he wanted to be good at, in his career *or* at home.

"Should I go on?" Bob asked quietly.

"That was more than sufficient," said Ken. He looked out across the water and felt the salt sting his skin. "Those were painful questions to hear, but they were dead on. You've opened my eyes."

Then a new reality dawned on him. "How am I going to find all that time to practice, on top of everything else I have to do?" Ken asked.

"Right now, you're like most people, putting your head down at work, getting through the day, not finding much time to deliberately practice—right?" said Bob.

"Uh-huh." That was a fair assessment.

"Well, what if you spent just one hour a day practicing one thing that you want to excel at? Could you fit in just one hour?"

Ken's first reaction was that it was impossible, but then he added up the minutes he spent each day on things that didn't really lead him anywhere.

"You know, I probably spend at least an hour a day surfing the Net fairly aimlessly or flopped in front of the TV," he finally replied.

"What kind of benefit do you think you'd see if you deliberately practiced one thing for an hour every day instead? Do you think that pretty soon you'd see improvement?"

"From what you've said about the research, yes. And when you put it like that—just one hour a day—it is doable."

"It doesn't end there," replied Bob. "Already there are opportunities for deliberate practice right under your nose—you just haven't noticed them till now. In fact, your whole life is an opportunity for practice. The key is converting the *doing* into *practicing*. It is just a matter of stepping back on a regular basis and taking a few minutes to look at how well you're doing.

"Have a regular schedule for stopping and critiquing yourself. You might stop hourly, every several hours, every few days—whatever works for you. The important thing is that you *assess how well you did and how you can improve next time you perform a similar task*."

"Just like a coach might do with a player," added Ken.

"That's right, because remember, constructive feedback is a crucial part of deliberate practice," said Bob. "You can give yourself that feedback. Or when you have a meeting, you could ask your boss or someone you trust to note a couple of things you did well and a couple of things you could have done better on."

"It sounds simple. If I do this, will it really make a difference?"

"It's never going to be the same as my granddaughter practicing her violin 20 hours a week, or all that time Gretzky spent on the ice—but it's mighty effective, Ken. "Think about it: If you're changing your focus so that you're *practicing* even while you're *doing* your everyday job, the tasks you're doing become a way to improve your skills. Tick"—he made the gesture in the air with his index finger—"They're certainly repeatable. Tick. You can give yourself constructive feedback or call on someone you trust at work to coach you. Tick. Finally, you said yourself that work is hardly what you'd call fun, so that's a tick.

"In fact, I suggest that you actually *volunteer* to tackle the tougher stuff, within reason. Because if you choose something that's just challenging enough, it's a chance to learn and to stretch yourself."

It clicked for Ken. "I see what you mean," he said. "When we started out tacking, I noticed you sped up in stages, gradually putting more pressure on me. And actually, I do feel like I stretched past what I thought I was capable of."

"Gradient stress."

There seemed to be a name for everything, thought Ken.

"Think of the stress of performing a task on a scale from 1 to 10," said Bob. "When we started out tacking across the sound, your stress level was probably between 2 and 4. That's what is called the *stretch level*, where you're being pushed just a little out of your comfort zone. When you got used to it, that became your new level 1, or no real stress. Would that be fair to say?"

"It would," Ken said.

"Then I picked up the pace, pushing you to somewhere between 2 and 4 again, right?"

"Yes, I hadn't thought of it like that, but yes, that's what you did."

"So, when I handed you the tiller, how would you have rated that stress?"

"Oh, at least a 5. Maybe even a 6 or 7," Ken admitted.

"That was what I'd hoped," Bob said, nodding. "That's called the *strain level*. Pushing yourself to that level of stress is good for you, so long as you have the right support—a coach, a colleague, a family member, a mentor, a sharp friend who's willing to give you the unvarnished truth."

"Or a darn good sailor with at least 10,000 hours of experience," chipped in Ken, smiling his appreciation.

Bob bowed his head in acknowledgment and said, "But be warned, if you push above that level, you reach the breaking point. Challenge yourself to an extreme degree, and no matter how much support you have, you won't be able to handle the stress."

Ken remembered Carlos's and Pat's advice about starting out small, and it took on even greater significance now.

§

They were almost at the rocky island, and Ken could see that there was a small structure on it, a weather-beaten gazebo, with just a couple of old rocking chairs, a hammock, and a grill. Nearby were a few other islands, all of which had huge homes on them, with landscaping and swimming pools. It would have seemed to make more sense if Bob had headed to one of those, rather than this strange pile of rocks. But he docked the boat, and they tied it to a little wooden jetty. The two men got off the boat and began to scramble up the rocks toward the gazebo.

Ken couldn't help but think of the opportunities to learn and improve that he had missed in the past. And now he thought of all the people who *had* grasped such opportunities. There were many people light years ahead of him, and he found that discouraging.

Bob slowed down so that they were side by side, and it was as if he knew what Ken was likely to be thinking and feeling right about now.

"You know, Ken, I used to compare myself to other

people all the time. But in the end, I realized that wasn't very useful, because there was always someone better than me." From Ken's expression, it was clear he was amazed that someone so powerful, so well respected, should ever have felt that way.

Bob continued: "It was only once I started comparing me to me that I finally 'got' it and started truly achieving. Maybe you'll also find that it's more useful to compare you to you. What matters most is that you become 1 percent better than you."

It's more useful to compare you to you. What matters most is that you become 1 percent better than you.

Ken had to look down to find his foothold on the rocks. Bob said, "You can't start this journey from where someone else is standing, up ahead of you. You can't start from where you think they'll be next. You can't even start from where you'd like to be." Bob pointed to where they were heading, and then back down at the rocks beneath their feet as he said, "You have to start from where you are.

"You can think about tomorrow, and maybe dream a bit about the future—but doing your best in the present has to be the rule."

"What about the power of positive thinking? Do you think that's important?" asked Ken.

"Hope is good, but if you don't follow through with action, it's not a particularly useful strategy," Bob replied. "Too many of us think the positive thoughts but don't put into play a plan that forces us to take the actions that will get us to what we're dreaming about. *You can't just wish—you have to do.*

"Let me give you an example," Bob continued, as they reached the top and took their seats in the shade, looking out across the water; it had been worth the climb. "I heard Colin Powell speak once, and he told the story of a brand-new second lieutenant who was very ambitious and wanted to be a general. One night at the officers' club, the new lieutenant noticed a general at the bar and went up to him and said, 'Begging your pardon, sir, but how does one become a general?'

"'Son, you've got to work like a dog,' the general answered. 'You've got to have moral and physical courage. There may be days you're tired, but you must never show fatigue. There are times when you'll be afraid, but you can never show fear. You must always be the leader.'

"The lieutenant was so excited by this advice. 'Thank you, sir,' he said. 'So this is how I become a general?'

"'No,' said the general. 'That's how you become a first lieutenant. Then you keep doing it over and over, and eventually you'll become a general.'"

"So the key to reaching your goal is knowing where you want to go and which actions you need to do to get there—and then persistence and effort will get you there."

"Yes, Ken, that's it." Bob ran his hand over his short

white hair and gave a sigh. "It meant a lot to me at the time to hear that story, because I was actually pretty desperate. I was looking for answers.

"This was years ago, when you were just a kid," Bob went on, after eyeballing Ken. "I'd created a business, expanded fast—soon *I* was one of those people that other people compare themselves to.

"Then the business ran into financial trouble. I prided myself on being able to pay my vendors within 30 days, but I looked at the books and suddenly realized I couldn't. My net worth was suddenly significantly in the minus territory, Ken. My first marriage was falling apart. My kids wouldn't talk to me. Then a freak storm came through and wrecked my boat. I was on the verge of giving up. Never been so low in all my life.

You have to start from where you are. Doing your best in the present has to be the rule.

"Powell emphasized the need to *do your best in the present.* That really hit home, and I knew that's exactly what I had to do. I contacted all my vendors and came to an arrangement to pay them off gradually. I made a solid plan to not just recoup my business but take it to a whole new level in the long term," said Bob.

"I'm not saying it was a piece of cake. There were days I prayed that one of those creditors would run out of patience and push me toward bankruptcy so I could walk away from all the hard work. But I got out of bed every day and kept slogging.

"Doesn't matter who you are, slogging is sometimes what it boils down to, Ken. When I was going through all this, I'd talk to my friend who had a lot more to lose than me—and he did. He lost his jet and his interest in an NFL team. Because of a real estate crunch, his assets were losing value at the rate of a million dollars a month, which made my debts look like small change.

"I'd also talk to my brother-in-law, a landscape gardener whose business was flat. He was stressed because he was struggling to pay his family's car payments, which were about $400 a month.

"And you know what? The dollar amounts were irrelevant. We were all feeling the pressure, and we all had to do the same thing: First, sit down and find out exactly where we were. I had to really examine where I was and where the company was. It required a brutal assessment of the facts, which I had conveniently ignored for some time. I had grown complacent and overconfident. I had to learn to embrace exactly where everything stood. Once that was in hand, I had to make a plan, put my head down, and slog every day until I'd achieved what I set out to do."

"Must have been tough," observed Ken. "Is that the toughest thing you've ever done?"

"Nope, the toughest thing I've ever done was ask a friend for help—a different friend than the one in the real estate crunch. I'd always done things myself. Independent type. I believed that I could just figure out everything by myself. That, of course, turned out not to be true. I sought advice, and it was instrumental in helping me make a brutal assessment of my business and put together a plan to get out of the mess I was in.

The toughest thing I've ever done was ask for help.

"Of course, once I'd asked for help, I kind of thought someone would come and bail me out—another not-very-helpful belief. Then I very quickly realized that when you're in the midst of something like this, seeking outside help is wise but that you can't count on others to do everything for you. No one is coming—you're it."

No one is coming.

Bob looked around the small island. "I came out here a lot in those days—to think, to plan, to prepare for action—and as a break from the daily grind."

"And those plans you made, the slogging you did, the hours of deliberate practice . . . they're what made you the success you are today," said Ken quietly.

The older man gave a silent nod and looked directly at Ken. His message was clear: *You can do it, too.*

5

THE 30-DAY FORMULA THAT WILL CHANGE YOUR LIFE

As Ken gave his name to the receptionist to let the next One Percenter know he'd arrived for their appointment, he was tempted to stop and say, "Something's come up, I have to go." Then he thought of the raised eyebrow he would receive from Coach Jim, and he took a seat in the waiting room.

Almost a month had passed since the sailing trip. A sense of dissatisfaction with the process had taken hold of Ken after he'd learned how many hours of practice it took to become truly great at something. Ken had appreciated Bob's time and trusted that everything he had said was true, yet he felt a certain resentment. Sure, Coach Jim had said there would be challenges along the way—but 10,000 hours of challenges? Just so he could be 1 percent better? So far, the results of his attempts at change had been patchy, and that made him question his commitment even more.

The next One Percenter was Kris, a psychologist who ran a busy clinic that helped people maximize their capacity to learn—"kind of like a brain gym" was the way the soccer coach had explained it. Ken wasn't sure what he was even doing here, but he figured that this next appointment could at least be an opportunity to formally bow out of the process. After all, it wasn't as if he'd signed a contract, he told himself.

Ken knew plenty of people who were just like him and who were getting on with their lives just fine. They didn't feel the need to go on a big program of change and improvement. Ken decided he would simply try doing what most of them did: He would make the best of things and count his blessings, and each year he would make New Year's resolutions to work on certain aspects of himself that he felt needed improvement.

That was the plan he laid out to Coach Jim when he finally faced him at his son's soccer game. Ken had tried to rush his son to the car straight afterward, as he had for a few weeks in a row, but Jim wasn't having any of that this time. He strode across to Ken before he'd made it to the parking lot. Jim told him he'd had a call from Kris, who was wondering why she hadn't heard from Ken.

That's when Ken became acquainted with the soccer coach's raised eyebrow. Jim reminded Ken about the commitment he had made to the ground rules, and of Ken's initial energy and enthusiasm for The One Percent Solution. Finally, Ken agreed to meet the next One Percenter.

He had written up notes immediately after the sailing trip with Bob but hadn't looked back at them. Now he thought he'd better have his ducks in a row, so he opened up his notebook and looked at what he'd learned:

1. To become the best of the best takes 10,000 hours of deliberate practice.
2. Everyone who spends time in deliberate practice improves their performance.
3. Turn daily tasks into deliberate practice by:
   a) assessing how well you do a task and how you can improve next time
   b) getting constructive feedback
   c) tackling goals that are challenging but achievable with support.
4. Compare yourself to you, rather than to others.
5. Plan ahead and set goals, but do your best in the present.

§

Ken had expected Kris to be disappointed or even angry with him for questioning the process that she was committed to. He was pleasantly surprised when she offered him a comfortable chair and a cup of tea—and a friendly ear. She told him that Coach Jim had filled her in on the basics of how Ken felt, and now she invited him to tell her in his own words. She sat opposite him, looking relaxed and attentive.

"Kris, I can see that The One Percent Solution has worked for you and the others in the group—but I just don't have thousands of hours to spend practicing," he said. "And even if I did have a spare 10,000 or so hours, what's the point if it's only going to give me a 1-percent edge?"

"It seems that it might help if you begin to look at this process of improvement within a more relevant time frame," she began. "Carlos tells me that you play golf every now and then, right?"

"Maybe once a month," Ken replied.

"Okay, to be good enough to win the British or U.S. Open or the Masters would take at least 10,000 hours of deliberate practice on the course—agreed?"

"Yes, I did some reading after my session with Bob, and I can see that the evidence has proved that," Ken replied.

"The prospect of all that practice is daunting, I understand," said Kris. "But let's say that you started taking regular lessons, committed yourself to playing a round of golf at least once a week, and spent just an hour a day practicing your swing, watching training videos, and reading training books.

"I'm willing to bet that in Week One you would see *at least* a 1-percent skill improvement compared to now."

"Yep, I think that sounds about right. And I get it that a 1-percent improvement is better than nothing—but really, I can't see how it's worth all that practice if you still get only a 1-percent improvement."

"Perhaps you need to look at this with a longer lens, Ken. Let's say you keep up your new routine and you improve by another 1 percent the next week." She paused and let him absorb this idea, then added, "That second week's 1-percent improvement wouldn't be an improvement just on your original skill level. You were already 1 percent better, so now you would be improving on your improvement, wouldn't you?"

"Kind of like compound interest in my bank account, you mean?"

Kris smiled. "Yes, you could look at it that way. Just as you increase your savings power by earning interest on your interest, there is a snowball effect to improvement, too. Keep paying into your skills bank with deliberate practice, and you will see continuous, growing improvement. At the end of, say, three months or six months, you wouldn't just be 1 percent better than you were at the start. You'd have gone way beyond that," said Kris. "And if you make deliberate practice a part of your life, there is no end to this compounding improvement, Ken."

"That's an attractive prospect," he replied, "but I'm still not sure that this is the easiest or the fastest way for me to get the results I want."

"So, Ken, do you have another strategy in mind?"

"Yes, actually, I've already written down my New Year's resolutions," he said, flipping to a list in his notepad and raising it for Kris to see. "These are the changes I am going to make starting January 1st that will improve my career, my family life, my health, and my fitness. This strategy will bring me immediate results, and then the following year, I'll tackle another set of resolutions, until I'm done."

Ken thought the psychologist would be impressed by his planning, but her expression was neutral as she looked at him, her head tilted to one side.

"I applaud you for your good intentions, Ken," she said. "It's great that you have a strong commitment to being a better person—for yourself, your family, your friends, and colleagues. But before you choose that approach, would you like to hear about the research that has been done on the effectiveness of New Year's resolutions?"

"That would be really helpful, thanks," answered Ken.

"New Year's resolutions rarely work," she said.

"For instance, a psychologist by the name of Richard Wiseman, a professor at a university in the U.K., looked at the outcomes for people who had made New Year's resolutions. Ken, 88 percent of those people failed to keep their resolutions.

"That means your chance of sticking to the resolutions on your list is just a little more than one in 10."

"Oh," he said. If he was a betting man, he wasn't sure he'd back himself at those odds.

"That doesn't mean that it's impossible to change for the better, or that I doubt your ability to change for the better," Kris reassured him. "What it does mean is that New Year's resolutions are one of the least-effective ways to bring about lasting improvement.

New Year's resolutions rarely work. Eighty-eight percent of people fail to keep their New Year's resolutions.

"And it's not just that they're ineffective," she added. "They can also be psychologically damaging."

Ken replied, "How could something positive like a resolution to be a better person be damaging?"

"The resolutions most people make generally fall into the same categories each year—weight, fitness, careers, relationships, money," replied Kris. "The trouble is, the goals are often very broad and are almost impossible to achieve all at once and all of a sudden. Yet that is precisely what we ask ourselves to do when we set a resolution. Do you think any of the resolutions on your list could be described that way?"

Ken looked at them again, and he had to say "Yes." He had gone for big changes that would bring turbo-charged improvements in his life—or so he'd thought. "What you're saying is that it's almost as if New Year's resolutions set you up for failure," he said.

"Yes, Ken. And when we fail to achieve a goal, we tend to lose our sense of self-control. I'm sure you've known people who say they will never eat another piece of chocolate or smoke another cigarette after January 1st. They lose a pound or have a smoke-free week—and then all of a sudden they're putting on even more weight, or they're running out for a cigarette twice as often as before.

"Most of our resolutions involve some aspect of our self-esteem, so that takes a beating, too. We may become dispirited and feel down—maybe even hopeless. That's the damage I'm talking about."

Ken leaned toward the coffee table in front of him and picked up a brightly colored stress ball. He sat back and squeezed it repeatedly as he thought about what the psychologist had just told him.

"Why does it have to be so difficult to change?" he asked. "Maybe it's all in the mind, and those people who failed to keep their resolutions just weren't disciplined enough. What if they simply didn't have enough willpower?"

"That's it, Ken. It *is* mostly in the mind, and you've hit on one of the major reasons that resolutions usually fail: a worldwide shortage of willpower.

"By the end of the first week of January, only 75 percent of resolution makers have stuck to their resolutions. That means one in four people don't have enough willpower to last for even seven days. As the weeks go by, more and more people's willpower gives out. In fact, those who rely solely on willpower are among the least successful at making lasting changes."

> By the end of the first week of January, only 75 percent of resolution makers have stuck to their resolutions. That means one in four people don't have enough willpower to last for even seven days.

"But what if *I* just really set my mind to it?"

"A handful of people do stick to their resolutions—but very rarely do they succeed because they just set their mind to it," she said, taking a model of a human brain from a shelf beside her.

She held it up, pointed to the top front, and said, "The part of the brain mostly responsible for your willpower is here, just behind your forehead. It has quite a few jobs to do: It also keeps you focused, handles your short-term memory, and solves complex problems. Asking it to exert willpower to suddenly change an old habit is often one job too many.

"That's partly because brain chemicals acting on the

brain's reward and motivation system deep within"—
now she pointed underneath—"do such a good job of
setting up habits. You unconsciously do things the same
way each time. It would simply be too exhausting to
have to make a conscious decision about everything you
do. Just think of the way you brush your teeth."

Ken went through the actions in his head and realized
that he started in the same place and followed the same
routine each time.

Kris put the model back on the shelf. "Now let's try
a little exercise," she said. "Put your arms out straight
in front of you and clasp your hands together, with your
fingers interlocked." Ken did as Kris said.

"I see that one thumb is on top," she said.

Ken looked, and said, "Yes, it is."

"Now unclasp your hands and re-clasp them so that
the other thumb is on the top."

He did so, and she asked, "How does it feel?"

"Weird," said Ken. "I never realized that I would
automatically favor one way of bringing my hands
together. And now I've done it a different way, it feels
unnatural and . . . awkward."

"You can relax your hands, Ken," Kris said. "Now
I want you to think back to the times when you tried to
make that change Carlos encouraged you to make for a
month. How did you feel when you tried that?"

"Actually, I felt a lot like I did just now. The new
way of doing things didn't come naturally to me," he

admitted. "I've always thought it was important to be true to myself, and when I tried a new way of acting, I felt like I was being someone else. I felt uncomfortable."

"That's good, Ken," she said.

He looked puzzled.

"Ken, knowing the way our brains are wired, I'd be worried about your mental health if trying a new way of doing something didn't make you feel uncomfortable. The question is: Did you work through that discomfort? Did you maintain the change for at least a month?"

Looking a little shamefaced, Ken replied, "Because it made me, and some other people, feel uncomfortable, I started to skip days. And the more days I skipped, the harder it became to start again."

"So, you more or less returned to your old habit?"

"Yes, that's probably fair to say. For the most part, things just seemed to naturally settle back to their old level."

"Was it a bit like the temperature in your home, which might fluctuate a little but returns to the same point set by the thermostat?" Kris asked. He nodded, and she continued, "We do the same, Ken. We tend to ease back to a certain set point that we've become used to—a point where we're comfortable."

"Sometimes it seems pointless to try and fight it," said Ken. "Perhaps the most sensible thing for me to do would be to stop wasting energy trying to improve all these things that are difficult to change. If I spend hours practicing anything, perhaps I should practice being happy with the life I have."

"Are you sure about that, Ken?" Kris asked. "The fact that you came here prepared with New Year's resolutions was actually an important clue for me. Research has also shown that the less happy you are, the more likely you are to set New Year's resolutions."

She was quiet for a moment, giving Ken time to remember the feeling he'd had right at the start of the process, when he'd woken up and realized that he truly wanted, and needed, to make changes in his life.

"We tend to hold on to things for too long," continued Kris. "Out-of-date versions of our self-image, old hurts and resentments, limiting beliefs about our abilities to succeed and to change."

Ken thought of several examples in his own life.

Then Kris asked, "Have you seen what happens when someone takes a baby from its mother's arms?"

"Oh, both my kids went through a period when if they were handed over to the babysitter, they cried—I mean, *really* cried," Ken recalled.

"Would you be surprised if I told you that most of us still feel a version of that panicked baby response? You might not actually kick and scream like a baby, but inside, that's often what happens when you're faced with change—even when you're the one making the change.

"That kicking and screaming baby response may have been a useful one as an infant, but it's time for you to let that go," Kris said.

Many times Ken had struggled against change, even positive change. What a relief it would be to let that resistance go, he thought. "But if willpower isn't all that reliable and our brains are set up so that we unconsciously do things the same way each time, can I really change?" he asked.

Kris signaled to Ken to toss her the stress ball. "The good news is that your brain can be reshaped, just like this stress ball," she said, squeezing it. "That's because of *neuroplasticity*. Your brain is *plastic*, in the sense that you can mold it." Kris tossed the ball back to Ken. "When you learn or do something new, your brain grows new connections. It physically changes to deal with the new tasks you give it. The key to making a lasting change in the way you do things is knowing the optimal way to encourage those new connections."

When you learn or do something new, your brain grows new connections.

"I'm hoping you can show me the way," Ken said, and smiled.

"It's surprisingly simple," she said, smiling back. "Choose one habit—a way of doing something—that you want to change. Make it a small and specific change. If you make it too broad or difficult, you risk failing and ending up dispirited, as with the grand New Year's resolutions we talked about."

"Once I've chosen the change I want to make, what then?"

"Adopt this new way of doing things *every day for 30 days*. At the end of 30 days, it will be a habit that is automatic to you."

"Really?"

"That's right, Ken. It won't take anywhere near as much conscious effort after that. And then, you can move on to tackle another small change, practice it every day for a month, then move on to the next. Each year you can permanently change at least 12 aspects of how you live and work, Ken. And you can keep going for as long as you wish to keep on improving yourself and your life."

"Where does the magic number of 30 days come from?"

"A man named Maxwell Maltz, who was an author and great thinker and also a plastic surgeon, observed that it took patients who underwent plastic surgery an average of 21 days to become emotionally accustomed to the change.

It takes a minimum of 21 days for your brain to get used to something new and form new connections.

"He also found that it takes a minimum of 21 days for your brain to get used to something new and form new connections. So a minimum of 21 days of conscious effort is required to establish a positive habit or break a negative one.

"In my experience, it is more helpful to think in terms of 30 days, because it is easier to fit into your calendar and keep track of. It gives you a chance to not only establish the minimum 21 days but to really cement the new behavior into your everyday life.

"Putting this in terms that Pat might use, what you're doing is exerting the outside force that gets you past your inertia and keeps you focused on the new pattern until it becomes ingrained in how you do things."

"Have you seen this work for people?" asked Ken.

"Every day I see it working for people who come into this clinic. I've seen it work for all the One Percenters. As a matter of fact, I have a great example of a change I made this way recently. A while ago, I might have been embarrassed for you to see the huge stack of psychology journals that had built up on my desk. Not only did it look messy and disorganized, but I really need to keep up with all the latest research. I'd let a week slip, then another week, and all of a sudden, the pile seemed insurmountable.

"I gave myself a month to develop a new habit: I kept up with new magazines that came in, while each night I took home a magazine off the old stack, read it, tore out any articles I wanted to keep and filed them, and recycled the rest. On Friday, I took a few extra for each day of the weekend. Two months later, the stack was gone. It's been maybe six months now, and the stack has never reappeared.

"In a way, this part of The One Percent Solution is like Woody Allen's great quote, 'Ninety percent of life is just showing up.' You just keep putting one foot in front of another, and pretty soon you end up where you want to be. It's about picking the term paper off a page or two at a time, or keeping the magazine pile down—it's about *consistently* doing those things that you know will get you where you want to go. Everyone who has succeeded at something has done this."

"Ninety percent of life is just showing up."—Woody Allen

Ken picked up his list of New Year's resolutions again. "So, are you saying that if I break these big resolutions into smaller, more manageable changes and tackle each habit one by one, for 30 days at a time, I will bring about lasting improvement?"

"Absolutely, Ken. If you insist on making New Year's resolutions, make a resolution to improve some aspect of your personal or professional life by at least 1 percent during January. Then lay out a program to help you do that, and practice it every day of January. By then, you'll have a firm foundation in place for that habit and can carry it forward."

"Do you have any tips for getting through that first 30 days?"

"Be sure to reward yourself along the way for

sticking with the new habit. Tell your friends about your goal, to get their support. Focus on how great it will be when you succeed, rather than on what will happen if you fail. Write down your new habit and keep a diary of your progress. If you happen to have two habits you want to change and they're closely related—like losing weight and exercising more—then it may be better to tackle them together. But otherwise, you have a greater chance of success if you address one habit at a time."

Kris gave Ken a moment to write the tips down in his notebook.

§

"My magazine pile is just one example," Kris resumed. "You can commit to change any of the ways you do things by 1 percent—including even the way you think and feel."

Ken looked up from his notebook, a little bemused. "But I don't plan ahead how I think and feel. I just react. How could I possibly control or change that?" he asked.

"The most obvious habits we have are actions," replied Kris. "Some are positive—let's say each morning you habitually brush your teeth and then you hit the yoga mat for 20 minutes. On the other hand, some of the actions you habitually do are negative ones—maybe you follow up your teeth brushing with a cigarette."

It just so happened that Ken wasn't a smoker, but he could think of several things he did habitually on a daily basis that were less than positive.

"Meanwhile, all the time there is kind of a running commentary going on inside your head, built up of mental habits that are just as strong as any other habit.

"Again, mental habits can be positive or negative," Kris continued. "While you brush your teeth, perhaps you think about the day ahead of you with self-confidence or a sense of purpose—or perhaps you think of it with anxiety or boredom."

"What you're saying is that there are many different ways to think and feel about myself or a situation, but that I get locked into thinking and feeling the same way all the time, like a habit."

"That's right," she said. "Ken, have you ever had a boss yell at or criticize you?"

Ken nodded—and smiled when Kris said, "Well, that proves you're normal then!

"Let's call that experience an *activating event*." She wrote the words on a big notepad. "How did it make you feel?"

"Angry, demotivated, and down, of course," he said.

"Let's call those feelings the *consequence*," Kris said, writing those words on the same notepad.

ACTIVATING EVENT (an event or life stress)

↓

↓

CONSEQUENCE (a feeling or action)

"I notice that you said 'of course.' Was there any other option for how you could have reacted?"

"Well, I guess I could have resigned," he said.

"Okay, now let me tell you about a part-time job I had in grad school with two friends of mine, helping to do research for our professor.

"He was a formidable man, known for his temper. Well, one day he came in and just exploded—screamed that he was disappointed in the standard of our work and our productivity.

"As soon as he was done yelling, my friend Cindy burst into tears and quit. It was clear to her that she was considered incompetent and could never win back the professor's respect, she told us later. Cindy ended up changing majors, even though her real goal had always been to become a psychologist.

"My friend Bill—well, he figured the guy had just got up on the wrong side of the bed that morning. Bill kept his head down and went on with his work the same way he'd always done it, as though nothing had happened."

"What about you, Kris?" asked Ken.

"I was shocked and upset at first," she replied. "I went out for a walk to collect myself. And I got to thinking about what the professor had said. Some of it was out of line—but for some of it, I could see his point. I went back to the lab and decided to try some new ways of doing the job. My innovations paid off, and what was meant to be a short research assistant job grew into a launching pad for my career."

"You all experienced the same activating event—but there were three very different consequences," said Ken.

"That's right. Most of us think that the activating event causes the consequence: Your boss yells at you, so you feel angry and depressed," Kris said. "But it's not the activating event that leads to the consequence. It's your *beliefs* about the activating event that make you feel and act a certain way." Then she added to her diagram so that it now read:

ACTIVATING EVENT (an event or life stress)

↓

BELIEF (a thought, opinion, or conviction)

↓

CONSEQUENCE (a feeling or an action)

"When you were born, you didn't have beliefs or opinions," she said. "You picked them up gradually—from your family, kids at school, experiences you had, and so on. You may have developed very different beliefs than my friends, or me, or anyone else. You unconsciously make sense of events through the filter of those beliefs."

"Kris, can you tell me how this relates to The One Percent Solution?"

"Because your beliefs make you feel and act a certain way, *your beliefs have the power to help you achieve your goals.* Or to block your progress," Kris answered. "To continuously improve and gain that all-important 1 percent, you need to step back and look at your beliefs and change them if they aren't working for you."

"Can you really change your own beliefs?" asked Ken.

"You sure can. Humans are the only species with imagination. That can work against you—for instance, look at the tragedy Cindy made of our professor's outburst. Or you can make imagination work *for* you. The key is the power of yet."

The key is the power of yet.

Kris gave Ken a moment to write this down, before asking him, "Could you tell me one of your dreams or goals that you have not achieved?"

He thought of several, and chose to say: "I'm not a millionaire."

"How do you feel when you say that?"

"A little bit down on myself."

"Okay, now try adding *yet* to that sentence."

"I'm not a millionaire yet."

A smile broke out on Ken's face. "That's amazing, Kris. Adding *yet* immediately changes my outlook. It makes me feel more positive and as though I should keep on trying. I can even feel it in my body—I feel a surge of energy and well-being."

"I'm not surprised, Ken, because there is a strong connection between mind and body. If you change your mind, you can change your body," said Kris. "In one study, people who practiced basketball free throws 20 minutes a day for three weeks showed 24 percent improvement. Nothing amazing about that—but people who didn't actually throw but spent those 20 minutes a day *visualizing* making free throws improved almost as much—23 percent."

"You mean like positive thinking?" Ken asked.

"Nope," said Kris, shaking her head emphatically. "They didn't just think 'good thoughts.' They mentally saw themselves take hold of the ball, step to the free throw line, bounce the ball a couple of times, set themselves, take the shot, and watch the ball drop through the net. The interesting thing is that from this research we know that as you go through such a visualization, the muscle groups involved in the action flutter through the same sequence as they would if you were actually doing it."

"If the mind changes the body, the body must surely be able to change the mind, too," Ken realized.

"Great point. And that means you can also use some simple physical techniques to change your outlook to a more positive, helpful one. I've got an exercise you can try right now, if you'd like."

"Yes, please."

"First, look down at your belt buckle." Ken did so, and Kris looked at her watch. When 10 seconds had

> The body can change the mind, and the mind can change the body.

passed, she asked him how he felt, his head still hanging down.

"I feel tired. It's been a tough week. And I'm back to feeling a bit flat again, to be honest," he said.

"Okay, raise your chin and breastbone up high." He did so, and she asked, "How do you feel now?"

"Wow, I feel the same way I felt when I added *yet*— lighter, more positive. Less tired."

"Any time that you're feeling discouraged—about anything you're striving for—try using this exercise and *the power of yet*."

Ken now understood why Coach Jim had made him promise to stick with the process. Now that he'd dealt with the hurdles Jim had warned him about, he felt stronger—energized.

"Kris, thank you, I'm looking forward to using these principles so I can make 1-percent improvements every day," he said. "But I did have that slip with the first change I had committed to make. Is that a problem?"

"In fact, it may be a good sign, Ken. Research has shown that people who successfully changed often slipped early on. The difference is, they viewed that slip not as a disaster but as something that strengthened their commitment. A slip doesn't need to become a fall."

A slip doesn't need to become a fall.

Already Ken was refining his goal for changing one habit by 1 percent, and planning how he would start doing it tomorrow.

HOW NOT DOING ANYTHING HELPS YOU GET MORE DONE

For two weeks, Ken had been sticking to the new way he was choosing to do one thing in his life, and he felt good about it. There had been times when it had felt like hard work, but now that he was being sure not to miss any days, his new habit was beginning to feel more comfortable. And the more comfortable and confident he became, the more positive the response became from those around him.

Ken had been setting aside a few minutes each day to read his to-do list from his session with Kris. He found that reminding himself of these aims helped him keep up his new habit. Now, as he sat on a bench waiting for Jeff, the final One Percenter, he read the list again.

TO DO

1. Practice your habit every day for 30 days, so it will become automatic.
2. Do the same for other habits, one at a time.
3. Be aware that beliefs determine how you feel and act in response to events:

ACTIVATING EVENT (an event or life stress)

BELIEF (a thought, opinion, or conviction)

CONSEQUENCE (a feeling or an action)

4. Reframe negative beliefs to help you achieve your goals.
5. Don't let a slip become a fall.

He smiled at that last one. It was undeniably good advice—and seemed even more so now that he was sitting at the base of a steep and rugged-looking mountain. It would probably be nothing but a hill to Jeff, a former Olympic triathlete who was now in training for an upcoming ultramarathon. Looking up at the mountain and casting his mind back over his sessions with the One Percenters so far, Ken felt excited that he would soon learn the final key to The One Percent Solution, because he was ready for whatever extra effort it took.

§

When Jeff arrived, it wasn't from the parking lot, as Ken expected. He trotted out from one of the mountain trails, with a backpack on his shoulders, sweat pouring from him—but smiling. The men shook hands and introduced themselves.

"How about a walk?" Jeff asked. "I should cool down."

"Great," Ken said, slung his own backpack over his shoulders, and walked alongside Jeff up the mountain trail. They chatted about Ken's progress with The One Percent Solution, and Jeff's training program.

"I don't get here all that often, but this is one of my favorite places to train," said Jeff, and Ken could understand why. The path was steep and physically demanding enough for a darned good workout. Ken had his eyes firmly fixed ahead—walking, pushing ever upward—and was working up a sweat. He was starting to really get into it, feeling good that he was managing to keep up with Jeff, and beginning to think that this challenge must be the reason Jeff had brought him here.

But once they reached a certain height, Jeff stopped and said to Ken, "Do you see why I suggested we meet here?" and pointed to the view to the right of them. Ken hadn't noticed that the path had taken them up around the other side of the mountain, and that stretching out beneath them was a deep blue lake surrounded by woods. An eagle was cruising overhead. "Wow," Ken said. He looked surprised.

"I'm gonna guess you're the kind of guy who's always on the go," said Jeff.

"That's right, Jeff," said Ken, and Jeff could hear the pride in his voice. "I have a lot of responsibilities, so taking a break feels like a waste."

"That's how I used to be," Jeff replied, taking a deep breath and watching the great bird swoop past.

"Used to be?" said Ken. "But surely you must be one of the busiest men around! You look like you must train a lot, and you have a family, and Bob said that you even run your own business."

Jeff smiled widely, and Ken realized how calm and centered he seemed. Perhaps he got a great deal of help. Or perhaps he was one of those people who slept only four hours a night and got stuff done when mere mortals like Ken were sleeping . . .

"Can I tell you a story?" Jeff asked, laying his hand on Ken's shoulder, and then Ken saw something else in Jeff's smile—the kind of understanding people get only from experience.

"Of course, please," said Ken, and the two men set off walking along the trail again.

Since middle school, he'd wanted to be an Olympic athlete, Jeff told Ken. He showed incredible dedication and made sacrifices that most of the other kids at school wouldn't have dreamed of. He trained every day, and then on the weekends, his parents would drive for hours from their small town just so that he could train with an elite-level coach. Later, they would give up their entire weekends so he could compete. And at college, there was no partying for Jeff, just a rigorous commitment to training and competition. At 22, he achieved his dream: to compete in the Olympics. He came in fourth, which only made him even more driven to be up on that podium when the next Games rolled around.

"A matter of seconds had kept me from a medal, about a one-tenth of a percent difference, and I thought the only way to close that gap was to get straight back into training—and harder than ever before," Jeff said. "Coaches tried to tell me I needed to schedule more rest time, but my theory was: 'If I'm not training, somebody else is.'"

Ken understood. He'd never be an Olympian, but he knew what it was like to feel that if he eased off from his efforts for just a moment, others would outstrip him.

"Pretty soon, I was shaving a fraction of a second off my time here and there," Jeff went on. "I felt pumped. Sure, all my joints were screaming, and one of my knees ached pretty much all the time, but I learned to ignore that. Until I went to Hawaii for the Ironman world championships.

"In triathlons, you taper down your training for about a month before a big race. I hated to do it, but I forced myself to. That wasn't enough, though. I didn't realize it, but the damage had already been done," Jeff said.

"I was in the lead for most of the race," he continued. "Then, during the last section, the run, my knee finally gave out. Suddenly it was like there was a knife stuck in there. I managed to finish somehow, but I was one of the last across the line.

"I had so many surgeries I almost lost count, and I spent hours in rehab, just to be able to walk again the way I used to. I went into a downward spiral. It wasn't just the physical injury, it became a psychological battle, too. I felt like my whole life was over if I couldn't be an Olympian any more. I pretty much gave up hope and let myself go. Stopped doing any exercise at all. Ate whatever I felt like," said Jeff. He gestured that they were to take some stairs dug into the side of the mountain, and they began to descend, toward the lake.

"I beat myself up because I'd been warned that my body had needed rest time between training sessions so that it could recover," he said. "I'd forgotten the Olympic motto: *Citius, Altius, Fortius*—swifter, higher, stronger. I'd tried to be the swiftest, highest, strongest—and right away—rather than working at getting better every day, step by step. I was like one of those guys you hear about shouting 'I want stress reduction, and I want it now!'"

"How did you get back on track?" said Ken.

"My dad was worried about how my life was going to turn out if I didn't get my backside off the couch, so he brought over one of his colleagues to chat with me."

The man introduced Jeff to The One Percent Solution. Eventually, Jeff began, one by one, to establish healthier habits, including scheduling rest breaks. He went back to school and got a business degree, and started training for shorter triathlons, building up gradually.

"I worked really hard, but I also took time out to recover. And little by little, I saw my performance improve—in triathlons, study, relationships, work, you name it."

Ken and Jeff had reached the bottom, and the lake was directly in front of them. Ken's leg muscles were burning, and shaking from the strain of descending. The two men gulped from their water bottles.

There was a small spring nearby, which fed into the lake via a stream. They had passed the occasional hiker or runner on the trail, but still, Ken wasn't expecting to see about half a dozen people submerged in the spring, steam rising up around them. Now he understood why Jeff had told him to wear swim shorts and bring a towel and a change of clothes. Ken and Jeff walked over, greeted the other runners and hikers, dropped their stuff at the edge, and sunk into the water—which Ken was pleased to discover was soothingly hot.

"When I started amateur triathlons, I knew I needed to strike a smarter balance between training and rest than I had before, so I went and visited the Olympic Training Center to see what I could learn," Jeff said. "The coaches there told me that their training schedules are all about knowing when to push and when to rest. They also have a special Athlete Recovery Center. And you know what one of the favorite parts of that center is for many of the athletes? The hot tub."

"Huh, I wonder why?" said Ken, grinning. He could feel the tension in his leg muscles—and in his mind—melting away in the hot water.

"The athletes go to the recovery center almost every day. Some of the methods are more high-tech than a hot tub, like compression suits," said Jeff. Seeing the questioning look on Ken's face, he added, "Air gets pumped through the sleeves and the legs of the suit to apply pressure. It keeps the blood circulating immediately after a training session.

"There's an aqua massage bed that runs high-pressure water jets up and down the body," he continued. "Healthy snacks, too, because recovery depends on getting the right nutrition. You need to get electrolytes and protein into your body within 20 minutes of completing a training session. There's a dry sauna and a steam room. Massage therapists, meditation, yoga classes."

"Really?" said Ken. "It sounds like a spa." He couldn't help but wonder if relaxing was really the best way to become elite at anything, let alone athletics.

"It might sound like a luxury, Ken, but all the research shows that *the top 1 percent always schedule recovery time into their day*," answered Jeff. "Usain Bolt's a great example. At the 2008 Olympics, he ran the 100 meters in 9.69 seconds and broke the world record."

"I saw that race," said Ken. "He was incredible."

"What's truly incredible is that three years before that, he couldn't break the 9.75-second barrier. He got his breakthrough when his trainers realized he wasn't having enough recovery time. Bolt was worried his speed would go down when they added rest periods to his schedule, but his time improved by 0.6 percent," said Jeff. "And that improvement—*not even 1 percent*—was enough to turn him from being an exceptional athlete into the fastest human being in the world."

"I can see how an athlete can't give his best performance if he's sore and burned out from training, but does any of this apply to someone like me?" said Ken. "My attitude is: The more hours I spend working, the more I get done. Period."

"Under pressure, most people stop relaxing,

exercising, and eating properly. They sleep less and work longer hours," said Jeff. "But that's a big mistake. For one thing, people who work 10 to 12 hours a day are more than 56 percent likelier to develop heart disease or have a heart attack than people who work less than 10 hours. The tragic thing is, it's not even worth it anyway, because beyond a certain point, spending extra time at work actually becomes counterproductive."

"Try telling my boss that," said Ken, with a wry smile.

"That's a great idea, Ken!" Jeff answered. "When I saw the benefits I was getting in all aspects of my life from scheduling recovery into my day, I studied the research.

"I learned that what sets apart the top 1 percent is that they cycle throughout the day between periods of concentrated effort and planned recovery. It's all about having the right balance of work and rest."

> What sets apart the top 1 percent is that they cycle throughout the day between periods of concentrated effort and planned recovery.

"What does that balance look like?" asked Ken.

"The very best in any field work in a focused way for no more than 90 minutes at a time, with rest breaks in between. They have a short daytime nap, get at least eight hours of good-quality sleep a night, and take regular vacations," said Jeff.

Ken took a moment to imagine how he would feel,

physically and mentally, if his life followed this rhythm of concentrated effort and planned recovery.

"Did Bob already tell you about that study of the brilliant violinists?" Jeff asked.

"Sure, where they were split into three groups according to their success, and it was found that success depended on how many hours they practiced—at least 10,000 hours to be in the top third," said Ken.

"Well, they are a good example of how adopting a rhythmic approach to work and rest can give you the 1-percent advantage," said Jeff. "You see, it turns out that their success also depended on how much and how often they rested. The top performers had a daily routine of practicing for up to 90 minutes at a time, with no interruptions but with breaks in between sessions. The players in the least successful group didn't even have a routine for practicing and resting.

"The top two groups slept an average of 8.6 hours a night, compared to the bottom group, which averaged around 7.8 hours. The top two groups also spent about three hours a week napping, while the bottom group napped for less than an hour a week."

"Are you kidding?" said Ken. "I just assumed the top performers would be those annoying people you hear about who only need three or four hours of sleep a night."

"Those annoying people are pretty much an urban myth, Ken. One sleep expert says that, rounded down to a whole number, the percentage of people who need less than five hours' sleep is zero. In fact, 95 percent of people need at least seven to eight hours of sleep to function normally. Most people who think they can get by on less are kidding themselves," said Jeff. "They're probably dosing themselves up with caffeine and sugar the next day—but no matter what, performance drops if you don't get enough sleep."

"Oh. I probably get only six hours, or six and a half hours a night," said Ken.

"That's about the average—but to achieve the 1-percent improvement you've been hearing about, you would do better to follow the example of the greats," said Jeff. "The other One Percenters and I aim for eight hours' sleep a night, because we want to be like those elite performers, fully prepared for another day of improved performance."

"What is it about sleep that improves performance so much?"

"Let me answer that with a question," said Jeff. "If you want to stay on the path to improvement, practice and learning are crucial, aren't they?"

"Yes, that's my understanding of The One Percent Solution," Ken replied.

"Well, sleep is when you process and consolidate memories, so to make use of the deliberate practice that you do as a One Percenter, you need to make it a habit to get a good night's sleep. You'll also see increases in creativity, problem solving, and the ability to take a long-term view.

"Without enough sleep, you see a rise in bad moods, impatience, difficulty focusing, and mistakes—just think of the accidents that happen in hospitals when doctors and nurses work very long shifts. You see less alertness and a drop in performance," said Jeff.

Ken now looked at some of the challenging situations he'd faced at work and at home in a new light. Perhaps just a couple more hours of sleep might have helped him deal with them more effectively. He said, "When I've had a few especially late nights in a row, sometimes it's a struggle just to get through the day."

"That's because you don't have enough physical and mental resources to draw on, so you end up having to work even harder just to hold your ground. You certainly aren't in a position to focus, learn, and improve," Jeff replied.

"Maybe getting to bed earlier will be the next habit I start after I establish the one I'm working on now," said Ken.

"Great!" Jeff replied. "After that, you might like to consider starting a new daily habit of 90-minute sessions of work with breaks in between, with one of those breaks being a nap after lunch."

"I don't know, Jeff. Sometimes I nap on a Sunday afternoon, but I always feel groggy for half an hour or so afterward," said Ken. "I can't be like that on a weekday."

"The secret is keeping your nap short," replied Jeff. "You pass through several stages of sleep, and in those weekend naps you probably stay asleep long enough to pass into the deeper stages that take longer to wake up from. But during the week, if you restrict yourself to between 10 and 30 minutes, you will stay in the lighter stages of sleep and will wake up feeling refreshed. A study in Japan showed that just 15 minutes of napping after lunch made people much more alert for the rest of the afternoon."

"That would be a great help, because I usually start to fade later in the day," said Ken. "But if I nap at the office, I feel like people will think I'm lazy, maybe even sick."

"I understand, Ken," said Jeff. "This is what I hear in most every company I go into. But when they start to make naps a habit and see their performance climb, they feel very differently. If you start taking short power naps and others see the edge it gives you through the afternoon, you might be surprised to find that the idea catches on."

"Where do people in the companies you work with nap, though?"

"Some of the world's highest-performing companies have set up recovery rooms, but I've also seen some creative solutions," Jeff said. "One executive, when he started to feel the pressure building up, would give himself a 10-minute 'executive timeout.' He even turned an old storage room off his office into a timeout space, with a recliner chair.

"If you have a door, you can close it at a certain time each afternoon—even hang a 'Do Not Disturb' sign on it—and then lean back in your chair for a nap. If you don't feel comfortable actually falling asleep in your workplace, it can help even to just lean back at your desk and simply close your eyes, after letting your coworkers know that you're taking yourself off-line for a few minutes.

"My nephew even naps in his college library. He was feeling overloaded with study, so I went and worked out a routine with him: He now hits the books for about 90 minutes, takes a nap on a couch in a low-traffic area for 20 minutes, then starts studying again. The other kids just laughed at him at first, but when they saw his grades improve, a few of them started to do the same thing."

"Why every 90 minutes?" asked Ken.

"It's all to do with your body's natural rhythms, which cycle between higher and lower alertness about every 90 minutes," Jeff answered. "You may have noticed that every 90 minutes or so you start to feel restless, it becomes harder for you to focus, and you become more irritable."

"I usually just force myself through it, or go get a coffee or a snack," said Ken.

"Next time, perhaps you could try listening to those signals your body sends you, and take a break for 10 minutes. You may be amazed by how much of a performance boost you get when you return to your tasks. Actually, speaking of breaks . . ." Jeff said, standing up as the group of hikers and runners on the other side of the spring stood and started getting out. Ken did likewise, and saw that they were all heading for a jetty on the lake.

One by one, they jumped in, most giving a hoot or a yell as they did. Jeff jumped in, and finally, Ken.

It took a second or so for him to register that it was cold—*really* cold! He gasped as he rose to the surface and began to tread water.

Jeff grinned at the shocked look on Ken's face. "Did I mention that at the Athlete Recovery Center the Olympians go straight from the hot tub into a cold pool? It increases blood flow and stops inflammation." The guy was flat out laughing now, and Ken couldn't help but join in. As his body got used to it, he realized that the change was refreshing and had given him a burst of energy.

"If you're like most people, you probably feel a bit guilty taking breaks and think you'll get less done in your day," said Jeff. When Ken nodded, Jeff went on, "Well, that has been proven to be false. A few different researchers have increased people's total break time, by between 20 and 35 minutes a day. Those people felt less fatigued and had fewer injuries, and even though their working hours dropped, their productivity didn't at all.

"Rest breaks enable you to recover, so that you don't get tired, worn out, and sick. That means you can perform at your optimal level day after day."

"I can see how that is crucial to The One Percent Solution," said Ken. "You can't possibly devote yourself to performing better every day if you're burnt out."

"That's right, Ken. I learned it the hard way," said Jeff. "The other key thing to remember is that rest breaks give you the advantage of being able to work *smarter*. Have you ever had the experience of working on a complicated problem for hours, and it just seems to get more complicated, not less, the longer you go on?"

"Oh sure, I get frustrated. I get a mental block," said Ken.

"That's because you need to take a break and think about something else."

"I know what you mean," said Ken. "I remember once when I was trying to figure something out, I gave up and went and bought a sandwich for lunch, and by the time I'd eaten it and come back to my desk, I saw the solution right there in front of me."

"Researchers call that time away 'incubation time,' and they've shown that it does help you to creatively solve a problem," said Jeff. "So it's important to schedule rest breaks into your day—preferably one in the middle of the morning, one in the middle of the afternoon."

Ken floated on his back, looking at the blue sky.

"What's the best thing to do in those rest breaks, Jeff?" he asked, bobbing upright again.

"For athletes, recovery usually means doing something passive, like sitting in a tub or getting a massage," said Jeff, "but for anyone who doesn't have a physically demanding job, exercise is one of the best things to do while taking a break."

"How come?"

"You do need to do passive things—meditation, listening to music, sitting down to a nice meal with family or friends—but researchers have shown that if you have a mentally demanding job rather than a physical one, too much passive recovery will actually make you feel even more tired. Exercise has been shown to make you feel less tired.

"Maybe it's walking around the neighborhood, going out at lunchtime to the gym, swimming before work—whatever gets your heart rate up and your muscles and joints working. Do it at least three times a week for at least 20 minutes and you'll start to see benefits."

"I know I do feel better when I'm fitter," Ken agreed.

Jeff gestured toward the ladder on the wharf, and Ken swam over and climbed out of the lake. Jeff followed, and said, "Regular vigorous exercise can actually have as much effect as antidepressants. Exercise helps you sleep better at night, cuts through stress, and it even helps your brain work more effectively—in fact, cardiovascular exercise actually triggers your body to produce new brain cells. If you can exercise outside in a natural setting like a nearby park, the benefits are even greater."

"How come?"

"There's a lot to look at and concentrate on if you're walking down a busy street—but being near nature gives your brain a chance to rest and restore itself. At the University of Michigan, they sent a group of students for a walk in a park and another for a walk on a busy downtown street. They tested them afterward, and the ones who'd walked in a park were in a better mood and had sharper attention, and even their memory was working better."

As they made their way over to their backpacks and dried off in the late afternoon sun, Jeff said, "There's one last piece to the rest and recovery puzzle, which fewer and fewer people seem to factor into their schedules. Vacations."

The hike, the swim, the sun—it all reminded Ken of vacations when he was younger, and how they had given the year a kind of rhythm. And had made him feel recharged.

"There always seems to be so much going on now that it's hard to find a time when the whole family can get away for a decent chunk of time," he told Jeff.

"And going by the general trend, I bet that even when you do, there's e-mails and text messages from work that bring your mind back to exactly what you need a good solid break from," Jeff replied. "What people in the top 1 percent know is that they need to carve out some time in their schedule for a proper vacation without interruption unless there's a real emergency."

"My job is kind of on the edge right now, and I just can't afford for things to slide while I'm away," said Ken. "It's hard for me to justify a vacation unless I can see a boost in performance."

"I have a great example that might just help convince you," Jeff answered. "At the accounting firm Ernst & Young, they found that a person's performance review was 8 percent better for every 10 hours of vacation time they took per month. And the more time they spent on vacation, the greater the improvement."

"I guess what I really can't afford to miss out on is the chance to achieve that kind of improvement in performance," said Ken.

"That's right. You know how I said I used to think 'If I'm not training, someone else is'? Well, now I realize

If I'm not recharging my batteries, someone else is sure to be recharging theirs.

that it's just as true—and even more important—that if I'm not recharging my batteries, someone else is sure to be recharging theirs. And if I let that happen, they will be *improving their performance* the next day, while I'll just be *getting through* the next day.

"Another thing I've found is that as you get further

into The One Percent Solution, time you didn't even know you had will open up for you, thanks to leverage and the 20/80 Principle. By using some of that time in planned recovery, you'll be able to continually refresh and recharge your energy. That way, you can continue, day by day, to keep on improving, 1 percent at a time," said Jeff. "For now, how about we ditch the stairs and go back around the base of the mountain instead?"

Ken looked at the trail, which was on level ground and shaded by tall evergreens.

"That sounds like just the kind of rest and recovery that will set me up for a high-performance day tomorrow," said Ken, and the two men shared a smile.

THE CIRCLE IS COMPLETE

Having completed the learning sessions with the One Percenters, Ken was pleased to discover that the journey certainly did not end there. In the five weeks since he had met Jeff, the principles of The One Percent Solution had taken root in every aspect of Ken's life, and his understanding had grown stronger day by day.

Ken made sure to regularly look at his to-do list, to check which principles he was doing a good job of applying and remind himself of those he needed to apply more consistently. Reading through the list he'd made from his session with Jeff, he was reminded of a number of habit changes that he planned to introduce step by step in the near future:

1. Cycle throughout the day between periods of concentrated effort and planned recovery.
2. Work in a focused way for no more than 90 minutes at a time, and have rest breaks in between.
3. Make at least 3 of your rest breaks each week 20-minute exercise sessions.
4. Nap during the daytime for between 10 and 30 minutes.
5. Get at least 8 hours' sleep a night.
6. Take regular vacations.

Ken placed his notepad on the bedside table and put on the red baseball cap for the first time since the night at the driving range. He walked over to the mirror, straightened the cap, and adjusted his collar—then chuckled at his reflection. Carlos would sure get a surprise when he walked in to dinner wearing the red cap.

Ken was looking forward to the dinner at Carlos's place, because he would be meeting all the One Percenters again, and it would be the first time he'd seen them as a group. He felt honored when Coach Jim called to see how he was doing and to invite him to be a part of this get-together.

He grabbed his keys and was about to walk out the door, but as he caught sight of his reflection again, something made him do a double take. Something was different.

He stepped in closer to get a better look, and smiled as he realized that something *had* changed, and for the better. It wasn't his hair. It wasn't his clothes. It was *him*.

§

Carlos was grilling up a storm on his patio when Ken arrived. The two men cracked up when they saw each other. "Snap!" Carlos yelled. He'd put his red baseball cap on for the occasion, too, and it was pretty clear from the look on his face that he'd been hoping to surprise Ken.

"Well, great minds think alike, right?" said Ken.

Carlos put down his tongs, strode over, and stretched out his hand to shake Ken's.

"Welcome, Ken. Really good to see you. Glad you stuck with the process," he said. Then, lightly punching Ken's shoulder, he added, "I knew you would."

Most of the other One Percenters were sitting at a big wooden table set up for dinner. Coach Jim stood up to shake his hand. So did Bob, who said, "I knew you'd see it through, too, Ken." Kris and Pat came over to each give Ken a hug. They both commented on how well he was looking.

He thanked them, glanced around, and asked where Jeff was. Just then, the triathlete arrived—to the cheers, whistles, and applause of Carlos, Bob, Jim, Kris, and Pat. Over the hubbub, Coach Jim explained to Ken that this was the first time they'd all seen Jeff since the ultramarathon he'd trained so many months for—and had won the previous weekend. Ken joined in the applause and added his voice to the cheers, and there were more handshakes and hugs all around.

The guests sat, asking Jeff about the race, as Carlos finished up at the grill and began shuttling dishes back and forth to the table. As Jeff finished his story about his win, chatting gave way to eating. "Carlos, you've done it again," said Bob. "Oh man, this is good" came from Coach Jim. "Mmm-mmmm" was all Pat could manage.

Carlos was the ultimate dinner host, popping up to make sure everyone's water glass was full, offering more salad or bread rolls. Steadily, the conversation built up again, and Ken was fascinated to hear each of these exceptional people give an update on what was happening in their lives. They joked and teased one another as they talked about the wins they'd had since they last got together and the promising developments that were unfolding. And they offered one another support for the challenges they were facing. As their eating slowed, and first one then another and another began to stretch and sigh contentedly, Ken realized that he was the only one who hadn't given an update so far.

Carlos jumped up just then to double check that his guests didn't need anything else, but everyone waved at him to sit back down. Most of them were looking toward the other end of the table, at Bob, whose expression had grown very serious. "Ladies and gentlemen, I think it is time." Now everyone was looking equally serious—everyone except Carlos and Ken, who simply looked puzzled.

That's when Bob and the others reached under the table, and each whipped out a red cap. As they put their caps on, everyone broke up laughing.

"I can't believe you guys!" said Carlos, genuinely touched. "I know there's a couple of you who got yours recently when you started out on the process"—he nodded at Ken and Jim—"but you others who were here before me must have just gone out and got them especially. You're the best." A cheer went up around the table for Carlos, everyone thanking him for the great feast he'd just put on, and for his friendship.

In the silence that followed, Ken cleared his throat and said—suddenly feeling more emotional than he'd realized he would be—"I want to give my special thanks to you, Carlos. Coach Jim sure was right when he said you were a great person to launch me on the road to learning about The One Percent Solution.

"And Jim, of course, it was you who first opened my

eyes, and for that I am forever grateful. Discovering that what separates the exceptional from the *exceptionally* exceptional is only 1 percent unlocked a world of possibilities for me. You showed me that though I will never be an Olympian, unlike a certain person"—here he looked pointedly at Jeff, and everyone chuckled—"I can have a winner's heart if I commit to always doing something better today than I did it yesterday. I can't be 100 percent better than the rest, but *I can be 1 percent better at hundreds of things.* That's powerful stuff," Ken said, and there were nods all around.

"And by the way, everyone, Jim was pretty humble before when he filled you in on his season as soccer coach, but let me tell you: Jake's soccer team has improved so much that they're in the finals next week." Everyone clapped. "More importantly, Jake and the other boys are developing the mindset of the One Percenter. They are learning the skills and attitudes they need for a life of ever-improving performance, no matter what career path they choose to follow."

"I think that is one of the greatest gifts you can give a child," said Kris, and everyone murmured their approval to Jim.

As they turned their attention once again to Ken, he continued: "Then I met you, Carlos. I had thought that the reason I found it so hard to get started on improving my performance was because I just didn't feel motivated. Thanks to you, suddenly I saw that the way to get motivated is to get up and *do something*.

"I was being held in place by inertia, but if I just got started by taking action, I would break that inertia. I would build up momentum, and stay in motion."

"All credit must go to Pat for that last insight, of course. I never was great at physics!" piped up Carlos.

"Yes, thank you, Pat," said Ken, giving her a respectful nod. "Let's also not forget that Carlos showed me that because action is such a strong motivator, I need to think deeply about my goals and choose my actions wisely, because the more I do something, the more motivated I will be to keep on doing it."

Pat joined in the discussion: "Whenever I feel that I might be focusing on tasks that don't lead to my goal, I hear Carlos's words in my head: *'There is no point in doing well that which you should not be doing at all.'*"

"Well said!" Then Ken paused for a moment, scribbling something onto a napkin. Everyone waited expectantly. "After Carlos showed me his diagram"— he held up the motivation-action diagram for everyone to see—"I thought I knew all that I would ever need to know."

"And then I met Pat, who introduced a whole new powerful idea: leverage. Now I make it a point every day to focus on small shifts in my actions that will produce large shifts in my results. I can already see improvements in my performance," said Ken. As he talked, Carlos handed him a couple of fresh napkins, and he drew another diagram, then showed it around.

20/80 Principle

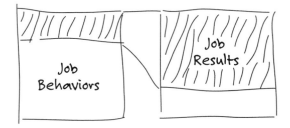

He looked directly at Pat and added, "I'm sorry for thinking you got the name of the principle wrong, by the way. I should have known that you'd be on top of that!"

"Oh, she pulled that one on you, too?" said Kris, gently elbowing Pat, who was sitting next to her. Bob rolled his eyes. Jim pulled the visor of his baseball cap down over his eyes for a second and shook his head.

"Well, okay, I guess I *could* explain the name change right at the start," Pat said, grinning, "but where would be the fun in that?"

"Hah, good one," said Ken. He stood up and leaned across the table, and he and Pat high-fived each other.

Ken felt himself turn more serious as he thought of his next stage in the process. He looked to the end of the table and said, "Bob, I have the deepest of gratitude to you—but I've got to say, it was tough to hear that there are no shortcuts to excellence."

Looking around the table, Ken saw that he was not the only one who had felt a little overwhelmed when they learned that

There are no shortcuts to excellence.

it takes 10,000 hours of deliberate practice to become truly exceptional at something.

"Of course, the take-home message really is that for those of us who want to continually improve our performance and become better each day at what we do, we need to spend time deliberately practicing.

"It's been a big help that you provided me with the tools I need to turn everyday tasks into an opportunity for deliberate practice, Bob: I've started assessing how well I do certain tasks and how I can improve next time. I'm in the process of identifying a couple of smart, trustworthy people I can ask for constructive feedback.

"You showed me that to learn and stretch myself, I need to set goals that push me out of my comfort zone, so long as I can achieve them with support. In fact, you really got me thinking. I hope you take this for the compliment it is: I actually drew up my own diagram to help me visualize and remember the idea. Would you like to see it?"

"You bet," said Bob, and leaned forward as Ken took another napkin and drew:

10	↑	Breaking Point
9		Breaking Point
8		Breaking Point
7	↑	Strain (Can handle with support)
6		Strain (Can handle with support)
5		Strain (Can handle with support)
4	↑	Stretch
3		Stretch
2		Stretch
1		Start

"This is great, Ken!" said Bob, impressed by the diagram, and proud that his words had had such an impact on Ken. "This is going to be a valuable teaching tool."

The One Percenters started passing the diagram around the circle.

"Awesome!" said Carlos.

"Thanks, this explains the idea so clearly," added Jim.

Ken continued, "Learning about gradient stress helped me realize that when I had set myself a goal in the past, I sometimes hadn't thought through what it would actually take to achieve it. I might have been sitting at a stress level of 1, my comfort zone, then set myself a very ambitious goal, not understanding that it would put me at a stress level of 5, 6, or 7 and that it would require outside support for me to achieve it. Or even worse, I'd set myself an extraordinarily high goal that might put me at 8, 9, or 10, which was virtually impossible."

"Your breaking point," said Pat, who had just been handed the diagram.

"It wouldn't matter if I had all the support in the world and put all my effort into achieving that goal, I simply couldn't," said Ken. He looked down and said, "I would become disappointed with myself. I'd feel defeated, like a failure."

"What would you do then?" Jim asked.

"I would lower my goals all the way down again, so that I was back at 1, with no stress. And once I did that, I was just treading water.

"Now when I set a goal, I look at this diagram and ask myself which stress level I will be at when I start working toward the goal. I aim for either the *stretch* level, between 2 and 4, or if it's something that I can get the right support for, from a trusted friend or coach or colleague, I aim for the *strain* level, 5 to 7.

"I also realized that as a leader, I need to watch the goals the people around me set. I need to make sure they're not setting themselves up for absolute failure and that I'm providing the right amount of support to help them learn and grow. I know now that in the past, I sometimes would insist on very high goals but then not provide the support to help them reach those goals."

"With your new attitude toward goal setting and support, you and the people around you will see results and won't get defeated and just give up," said Jeff. "Now, Ken, can I share something with you about the types of support you should look for?"

"Please do," Ken said, "I've been hoping for some pointers, actually."

"There are two main types of support to consider when you want to strain to reach a new level of performance," said Jeff. "The first kind works by removing obstacles that have been preventing you from stepping up to the new level. The second kind works by having a helping hand guide you up."

"How does that work in real life?" asked Ken.

"Here's an example: One of my friends is a swimmer who trains at the Olympic Training Center, and she took me to see the setup they have there at the pool. The Center provides both types of support.

"Most people don't know this, but those Olympic swimmers churn up so much water when they're plowing up and down the pool at training that the air right above the surface is filled with water droplets—just like mist. And all that water means that there's less oxygen for them to breathe."

"So you mean the harder they train, the less fuel there is available to power their bodies?" Ken asked.

"Exactly," said Jeff. "Imagine if you're already training at what feels like your maximum performance level, and then your coach asks you to perform just that little bit better—but without enough oxygen getting into your lungs.

"To deal with this, they blow air across the top of the pool to disperse those water droplets."

"That's amazing," said Ken. "And I see what you mean: That's a type of support that removes something that's holding you back from achieving a higher level of performance."

"You got it. There's another amazing thing they do at the Center when swimmers are ready to go to the next level. You know how weird it can feel to try to do something a new way?" he asked.

"Sure do," said Ken, and shared a smile with Kris.

"Olympians feel that way, too. So the coach will harness up a swimmer to a machine that tows her through the water at the faster speed she's aiming for, giving her a chance to get used to what that higher level of performance feels like."

"Awesome!" said Ken, imagining what he could achieve in the future by finding supportive people, organizations, and tools that could act in a similar way for him.

"With both of those types of support, once the swimmer has established the new level of performance, what used to be a strain"—Jeff had been passed Ken's diagram and now pointed to the 5 to 7 range— "becomes her new comfort zone."

"And she can start the process again, aiming for another performance target at the strain level—with support, of course," said Ken.

"Precisely," said Bob. "And can I just say, I'm glad to hear that you've started to do all those things you mentioned, Ken. Just don't forget, setting a goal and keeping it in sight is important, but the only way to get there is one step at a time. Plan ahead, but *do your best in the present.*"

"I hear you," said Ken, thankful for the reminder. "Now, Coach Jim and Kris both know that I hit a rough patch." He looked at each of them in turn, and they shared an understanding smile. "Kris, thank you for helping open up my mind so I could see the unlimited benefits of The One Percent Solution.

"You showed me that over the long term, the

benefits grow greater and greater. If I use the tools Bob gave me and deliberately practice the right skills, my performance will in fact improve exponentially, because I'll be improving on improvement."

"Absolutely, Ken," acknowledged Kris.

"And it turned things around for me when I learned that it was normal for change to feel uncomfortable or difficult, even when the change is positive.

"You also talked a little about how important it is to let go of some of our old ideas and ways of doings things. It can be a challenge to let go. It can be a challenge even just to realize that you're holding on to something and need to let go. So that's one thing that I'd be really interested to hear more about if anyone has any stories they'd like to share."

Jeff was the first to speak. "After my injury and all the operations and rehab, it took me a long time to accept that I wouldn't compete at the Olympic level again.

"When I learned about the power of letting go, I realized that to move forward in my life I needed to let go of my old idea of me, the Olympian. I realized my grieving had gone on too long. So I let go of the idea that my entire identity and value depended on my achievements in this one particular field.

"And when I let go, my whole future opened up in front of me. Now I'm happier and more successful than I'd ever dreamed, just because I was able to accept and embrace that new reality."

"You're an inspiration to all of us," said Pat. "I have a story, too. When I first started working from my home office, I thought everyone expected me to be Superwoman—which was certainly what I expected of myself.

"I had freed up all this time I'd previously spent commuting and in meetings, so I'd be able to do everything perfectly, I thought. I'd do more of my own research and have more scientific papers published. I'd be the fittest woman in my neighborhood, have the perfect house, be the best wife, and most of all, be the ultimate mom.

"As you all know, I ended up struggling to focus on the work I needed to get done, and scattered my energy all over the place. Those work shoes my sister gave me did the trick. But I also had to let go of this desire to be Superwoman. Once I let go of that expectation, I was able to focus my attention where I needed to, when I needed to. And of course, it's led to ever-increasing performance and success."

Bob now cleared his throat, turned to Ken, and said, "When my first business failed, I've gotta tell you, I was knocked off my feet and thought there was no way to salvage it. I was on the verge of declaring bankruptcy.

"Then I realized that it was time for me to let go of some of my ideas and ways of doing things. I'd prided myself on always paying my creditors within

30 days. Well, I had to let go of that pride.

"Once I let go, I was free to get on the phone to those creditors and tell them about the company's financial problems and how I was planning to fix the situation. And you know what, they didn't think any less of me—actually they appreciated my honesty and were happy to come to new payment terms."

"Thank you, it means a lot that you shared your stories," said Ken. He turned again to Kris and continued: "You also showed me the wisdom of changing something I do and sticking with the change every day for 30 days so it becomes automatic. I've already done that once, and I'm on to my next. For that, I thank you, Kris. So would my wife and kids if they were here, and so would the people at work and my friends—in fact, everyone I come across in a day.

"And there has been a boost to my performance since I learned that my beliefs—my thoughts—have the power to help me achieve my goals. I can change beliefs that aren't helpful, and I can use my imagination to visualize myself achieving my goal."

Ken paused, and turned to Jeff. "You gave me the last piece of the puzzle, Jeff, thank you. I now understand that to have the energy and resources I need to improve day by day, I need to cycle between periods of concentrated effort and planned recovery.

"You know how I mentioned that getting eight hours' sleep a night may be my next new habit to introduce? Well, that's the habit I'm working on now," Ken said. When Jeff praised him for taking action, Ken felt a bit uncomfortable. "Thanks, Jeff, but I don't want you to think I've got it all worked out," he said. "I'm not quite there."

"Yet," said Jeff.

"Actually, none of us are quite there yet, Ken," said Kris. "Makes life interesting every morning when you wake up, don't you think?"

Ken was amazed. "Surely I must be the only one who still feels like he's finding his feet. You're all so . . ." He gazed around the faces at the table, searching for the right word. "You're all so exceptional."

"Reality check!" said Jeff. "Okay, you know how I said my father linked me up with one of his colleagues who helped me understand how to balance work and recovery?"

"Sure," said Ken.

"Well, that colleague was none other than Bob here."

"Bob?" said Ken, unable to hide the disbelief in his voice. He associated Bob with deliberate practice, dedication, focus—not rest breaks.

Bob laughed and said, "And why do you think I got to be something of an expert on recovery in the first place? I damn near killed myself with work and worry!"

"I have to really remind myself to take breaks," said Carlos.

"Oh yeah, I've seen your calendar," Ken remembered.

"His calendar? Just take a look at *him*!" said the rather laid-back Jeff. Carlos had gotten up and was going around the table collecting empty plates—at lightning speed.

"Well, I have to be careful not to focus on the wrong tasks and leave the important ones till two o'clock in the morning. That isn't second nature to me," Pat said. "*Yet.*"

"And I haven't quite got the hang of changing unhelpful beliefs and visualizing myself achieving my goals . . . *yet!*" said Coach Jim, and they all chuckled at that.

Kris said, "Ken, The One Percent Solution isn't about suddenly achieving perfection—which is lucky, because perfection is unachievable. The One Percent Solution is about trying every day to be a little better than yesterday."

"And that *is* achievable," said Ken. He paused, then said, "All right, I know I've just said that it's a challenge to consistently apply the principles—but in some aspects of my life, the principles are working so well that I'm getting *more* than a 1-percent improvement. Is that okay?"

Everyone burst into laughter. "Of course you're getting better than a 1-percent improvement in some things, and that's perfectly fine," Coach Jim reassured him. "That's great, actually! Most everyone does get greater than a 1-percent improvement in at least a few of the areas they work at improving."

Bob took over from there: "We emphasize 1 percent because it's almost impossible for anybody to say no to trying for a 1-percent improvement, and also because we know that if you follow the principles, you are guaranteed to get *at least* a 1-percent improvement. You may get more—in fact, most people do get more. We had a sales rep who set a target to improve his sales volume by at least 1 percent a month. When he got rolling, he was regularly improving it by 2 to 3 percent a month.

"Even those huge goals you see are usually either the result of hundreds of 1 percent improvements or a change in action that because of leverage produced an outsized result."

"And it's all relative," said Kris. "It depends on the time frame you're using. The rate of improvement can look very different, depending on whether you view it over the course of a day, a month, or a year.

"It also depends on whether you're judging an improvement in one of your *actions*—the way you do something—or judging the *results* of that action.

"You can usually make a *change in action* in a relatively short period of time. If you're like most people, in just one day you'll see at least a 1-percent improvement in the way you do something.

"But you may need to wait a little longer to see a *change in results*. It may be a week, a month, a quarter, or even a year."

"It's like when you changed your habit with the magazines that were piling up on your desk," said Ken. "You changed your actions by each day reading any new journal that arrived and one from the old pile. Right away, you had at least a 1-percent improvement in your actions. But the ultimate result you were aiming for—a clean desk that stays that way—took a couple of months to achieve."

"That's right, Ken," said Kris. "The important thing is that at the start you sit down and think about the improvement you want to make to one of your actions, and the improvement you want to see in the results of that action. Then you need to decide whether you're going to achieve those improvements in a day, a week, a month, a quarter, or a year."

Ken looked around the table and asked, "The principles you've shared make so much sense to me. In fact, they're so simple and straightforward that I just want to check: Am I missing anything?"

"Ken, from all that you've said here today, I know that you now have the tools you need to live a life of excellence," said Bob. "You've begun to see that by following these principles, you can achieve at least 1 percent improvement—and often more. So I know it may be tempting for you to try to improve everything all at once.

"Don't try to be better in all parts of your life at

once. First, work to be just 1 percent better in one area and get that cemented in. Then work on another aspect. Pretty soon, getting 1 percent better won't be something you're working on, it will be just the way you are. *Do and then be.*

"I'm not saying it will always be easy. You will meet challenges. They're a natural part of life and of the process. And as Kris has shown us, we do tend to slip back to what's comfortable—even if what's comfortable isn't what's best for us.

"You may also be tempted to follow the way the people around you are leading their lives. It's not always easy to follow your own path rather than the crowd's. But believe me, Ken, the benefits of following this path are extraordinary. And infinite. There is no limit to the types of improvement and fulfillment that you can create in your life—and the lives of the people around you, because let's not forget, there is a ripple effect here."

Ken looked into the faces of everyone around the table, and by way of salute, lifted his cap. "I am so grateful to all you One Percenters," he said.

"What do you mean, *you* One Percenters?" said Carlos, grinning.

"Yeah, Ken, I think you mean *us*," said Coach Jim.

The faces around the table were all smiling, and now they took off their caps and saluted him, too.

§

A couple of times a year, Ken and a few of his longtime friends got together to catch up and kick back. This night, they had gone to David's place to watch a football game on TV.

Life hadn't been easy for Dave since the last time they'd seen one another. His marriage had ended, and he no longer had his secure job but was in the midst of a string of contract positions. The other guys told Dave how great it was that he was keeping a positive and upbeat attitude.

But beneath that, Ken thought he could see something else in his friend. From the look in his eyes, Ken sensed that Dave was at a turning point, unsatisfied with the way things were, and searching for a new way forward.

At the end of the game, the others left. Ken stayed put. As the sound of their friends' cars died away, Dave said, "Ken, your life seems to be going great right now, so it makes sense you're looking so well."

"Thanks, Dave, I *do* feel well," said Ken simply.

"But it's not that everything just happens to be going your way, is it? There's something different about you. Please don't take that the wrong way. You're still *you*, my old college buddy Ken—but you're the most confident, the most positive, the most together I've ever seen you. What's happened?"

"I'm really glad you asked, Dave," said Ken. "I've been on quite a journey. I've met some awesome people and learned some truly effective ways to live my life so that I can perform better and better every day. The results have been incredible."

Dave was leaning forward on the couch opposite, and Ken saw in his face the kind of light that Coach Jim probably saw in his own that day at his son's soccer game.

"Any chance of some coffee?" Ken asked. "I get the sense you're ready to hear more, and I think you're going to be interested in what I have to say."

ABOUT TOM CONNELLAN

When companies such as Marriott, FedEx, and Neiman Marcus want to take their performance to another level, they all turn to one man—Tom Connellan. And with good reason. He's solid. Every year, he keynotes scores of meetings.

A former program director at the Michigan Business School, Tom brings depth and breadth to your conference. As a company founder and former CEO, he knows firsthand what it takes to grow a business. Tom started a service company in the health-care field and built it into a network of 1,200 instructors serving 300 hospitals and most of the Fortune 500 firms. More than 1,000,000 participants went through the programs, and two different Surgeon General reports cited the firm's program quality. Tom knows what it's like to be on the firing line of business, because he's been there.

Tom is the bestselling author of ten books and numerous articles. He's been the editorial director of four management and human resource magazines. Tom brings solid content and a passionate delivery style to his presentations. He captures the audience's attention and holds it from start to finish.

Selling Power magazine named him one of seven "Tough Talking and Truth Telling" keynote speakers.

Because his keynotes are packed with actionable ideas, everyone leaves Tom's sessions with practical how-to's they can immediately put to work.

For information on Tom's schedule and availability, call 734-428-1580, visit www.tomconnellan.com, or write to 1163 South Main Street, Suite 306, Chelsea, MI 48118.

Acknowledgments

Every author says "I couldn't have done this alone," and every author who's not crazy really means that, because this is where we get to thank those who contributed to our book. For me, it's always a tough job because there are so many that I always worry about leaving someone out.

So here goes.

Svetlana Ivanova, M.D., Ph.D., Kirti Kalidas, M.D., N.D., Paula Noack, L.M., C.T., and David Reifsnyder, M.D., all—through their solid approach to integrative medicine—put heartfelt energy into the book. Thanks to each of you.

My program manager, Karen Revill, kept the office running smoothly in spite of the fact that keeping me heading in the right direction while I'm writing must be akin to herding cats. Thank you, Karen.

Cody Kennedy and Jaci Dodd provided support and guidance for virtually every word and were available most any hour of most any day when I needed guidance on a phrase or word. Thank you, Cody and Jaci.

My sterling editor Vanessa Mickan did another superb job of developing, editing, pulling together, and laying out the words you find in this book. She's so good, you wouldn't even know she's blonde. She found words inside me that I didn't know were there. Any deficiency is my responsibility; any clarity is hers. Thank you, Vanessa.

Michele DeFilippo of 1106 design did her usual great job on the dust jacket. Special thanks to Michele and her entire team. Thank you, Michele.

Amy Collins McGregor's and Bethany Brown's deep book industry experience and savvy marketing knowledge have proven to be invaluable. Many thanks to them and the entire team at The Cadence Group for their many contributions throughout the process of pulling this book together. Thank you, Amy and Bethany.

And finally, last but most certainly not least, to Pam Dodd, my patient wife, who—for the most part—tolerated the travails of pulling this book together, my thanks, love, and appreciation. Thank you, Pam.